HAVING GIFTS THAT DIFFER

*"...so we, though many, are one body in Christ,
and individually members one of another.
Having gifts that differ
according to the grace given to us,
let us use them...."*
—ROMANS 12:5–6

HAVING GIFTS THAT DIFFER

PROFILES OF ECUMENICAL CHURCHES

Peggy L. Shriver

With an Introduction by Martin E. Marty

Friendship Press • **New York**

Manufactured in the United States of America

93 92 91 90 89   5 4 3 2 1

Library of Congress Cataloging in Publication Data

Shriver, Peggy L.
    Having gifts that differ : profiles of ecumenical churches / Peggy L. Shriver ; with an introduction by Martin E. Marty.
        p.   cm.
    ISBN 0-377-00199-6 : $7.95 (est.)
    1. National Council of Churches of Christ in the United States of America.   2. Christian sects — United States.   I. Title.
BX6.N2S52   1989
280'.0973–dc19   89-1230
                                                                 CIP

CONTENTS

FOREWORD

Very soon after becoming General Secretary of the National Council of Churches in 1985, I became convinced that serious commitment to the development of a community of communions (a self-identity adopted by the Council four years earlier) required us to know one another much better.

I asked Peggy Shriver, the Council's Assistant General Secretary for Research and Evaluation, to gather and tell the stories of the various communions, because I knew she would do it with interest and empathy. As General Secretary of one of the Council's member communions (The Reformed Church in America) from 1977 to 1983, I had repeatedly felt that Peggy displayed a discerning understanding of the communions as they were — a research understanding if you wish — enriched by a deep and playful love of the churches in their kaleidoscopic diversity and fluidity. That's the way I wanted us to know one another.

The studies were written primarily for members of the Governing Board, many of whom have had only limited experience with Christian communities and traditions other than their own. The result is a practical guidebook for ecumenical encounter. In fact, these profiles of the various communions were prepared to coincide with a schedule of worship following the liturgies of the various traditions at successive meetings of the Council's Governing Board during the last four years. Those services of worship have been moving and deeply appreciated experiences. They have been enriched by these profiles which have given them additional depth and context. They can do the same for similar experiences in other communities.

The central thrust of each chapter is to convey the ethos of the community being described as that ethos is formed and expressed in its history, worship, doctrine, life and work. There is a pinch of structure to give body to the brew — and a dash of official ecumenical relationships to link it all together. The result is an ecumenical smorgasbord — a foretaste of the banquet we ecumenists envision in the end time.

One standard of quality for this smorgasbord is that each entree is authentic. It is true that one chef prepared them all, but each has had to be approved by the people who cook up the recipe everyday, i.e., the leaders of that particular community. A coincidental result is that small communions are treated with the same thoroughness as large ones — a quality that sets this smorgasbord apart from most others of its kind.

One disadvantage of such a methodology of self-definition is, of course, that the errors and partial visions and failures of the various traditions are not likely to be placed on the table with the same prominence as are the gifts. The reader should, therefore, not expect to find them here. Yet, the road to reunion cannot be walked without repentance and renewal. But never mind, that will happen as we share the feast of life.

This book, of course, can be little more than a menu — the feast itself is to be found in gathering with the people of God around the various tables described in these profiles. As General Secretary of the NCC, I have had the privilege of sitting at most of those tables — some for a snack; some for a banquet; some for the sacrament. Those occasions have been among the richest of my life. So... taste and see.

ARIE R. BROUWER
General Secretary
National Council of Churches of Christ in the U.S.A.

PREFACE

Most religiously-oriented people have at least a few sharp images that rush to mind when they think of a tradition different from their own: the Orthodox — beards, robes, icons, incense; Quakers — silence, simplicity; Baptists — the Bible and Baptism by immersion; Episcopalians — the Book of Common Prayer; Presbyterians — the Book of Church Order; Black churches — stirring preaching, prayer, and music; Methodists — social concern from hearts "strangely warmed." Within the Christian churches alone there are vast differences. This collection of profiles is limited to Christian churches that have affiliated with one another to express their intention to be ecumenical, that is, churches that desire to be open to one another and to recognize their kinship in the Body of Christ. One of the great riches of ecumenical experience is discovering the spiritual vitality in "having gifts that differ."

Although Christians have gathered in consciously ecumenical meetings for many years, they often have not learned the significant facts about one another's traditions and histories necessary to enlarge their understanding. A few years ago participant members in the National Council of Churches of Christ in the U.S.A. admitted that they needed to pay more careful attention to one another's stories if they were ever to deepen their life together as a "community of communions."

The Office of Research and Evaluation was encouraged in 1986 to prepare a set of brief sketches or "profiles" of each member communion (denomination) of the National Council of Churches to enable the churches better to understand and appreciate one another. Seldom was an assignment more welcome! As Assistant General Secretary and head of the Office of Research and Evaluation, I began to study the thirty-two member churches with increasing enthusiasm over a two-year period. Each church was asked to point the Office to resources for study, and a person from each communion was named to be a reader and critic of the final product. Church leaders seemed eager "to see themselves as others saw them," and therefore few wished to take over the writing task themselves.

Undertaking what amounted to a "crash course in church history," I was profoundly moved by the unique riches of each tradition, the often poignant and sometimes devastating stories of their historical roots, the common human strengths and weaknesses, the evidence of the Holy Spirit as balm and goad, and the centrality of Jesus Christ to all of them. One could be receptively appreciative of the spiritual logic of each tradition, while knowing that each Christian has to make choices among them and not simply embrace them all. As people and cultures differ, so it makes sense that religious bodies have gifts that differ. The tragedy of history is that even churches have engaged in fierce forced choices rather than recognizing with humility and grace that the Spirit moves where it listeth among us. Each has an insight that is a special gift of the Holy Spirit. Many have paid a costly price to protect it.

The least satisfying aspect of this entire project has been the attempt to arrange and classify these communions. To list them simply in alphabetical order would be to ignore the important affinities of the Orthodox churches, the predominantly black churches, or the historic peace churches. Grouping them by family or by the beleaguered term "mainline" leaves an unconscionable number of orphans or sideliners. Even the finally accepted classification does not follow a consistent rubric, and one can certainly debate whether several "American origin" churches are as homegrown as the name implies, when several of them began as seedlings. But the denominational development of the "American" churches owes much and contributes much to the U.S. ethos. This arrangement, therefore, despite its weaknesses, does offer useful insights as well as recognize some very natural groupings.

I am grateful to all those from each communion who assisted in this project and to readers who helped provide editorial clarity. Most of all I am grateful for the opportunity to have delved elbow-deep into these traditions, and to have worked and worshipped with outstanding Christian leaders from their ranks in the ecumenical movement, as I've known it through the National Council of Churches.

PEGGY L. SHRIVER

INTRODUCTION

"Getting to Know You," the theme of a song from the old musical *The King and I*, relates to the motive behind this useful handbook. The churches which make up the National Council of Churches have dealt with each other for years. Their delegates work together on issues of common concern. Their leaders understand how to deal with leaders in other churches. Their members include members of other churches in their prayers and list them as partners in God's work. But some of these delegates, more of these leaders, and most of these members know very little about the inner life of these colleagues and partners. This book sets out to help remedy the situation of "knowing very little."

Compare the denominations to families and tribes, which everyone tends to do. People may be aware that down the block there are people named O'Connor and Polcik, Brown and Braun. They will learn something more about them if they plan block parties together. But it would be curious if some of these families were to come together through marriage, or in business partnerships, or through contract, without becoming more familiar with those who would be close to them because of these arrangements.

The interest would not be idle curiosity, just as mere idle curiosity is not likely to sustain the interest of readers of this book. The idle will not be curious and the curious have no time to be idle about Christian denominations: there are more curious subjects in the American museum or display case than these churches. No, the interest would be born, in the case of families, and is sustained, in the case of these churches, out of much more practical interest.

For example, families and churches have many unwritten

1

rules or practices based on written codes or declared intentions which one must know if there are to be good dealings. Peggy L. Shriver goes into some of these written and declared matters. We do not think how webbed and complex our neighbor's or our own family or church are until we try to make sense of their ways. "The Trowbridges just don't *do* things like that." "After all that the Murphys have suffered, they have a right to act *that* way; you would, too." "They're all right, but would you want your daughter to marry one of them?" So it is with the churches: "That just isn't *done* in the Episcopal Church." "If you'd do *that*, you know the Greek Orthodox Archdiocese in conscience would have to withdraw." "*Who* are these National Baptists, that they have such power when it comes to electing our mayor?"

What people *do* in one church body; *that* which we can or cannot do together; *who* that "other" is — these italicized words signal complex histories, statements of polity, and patterns of belief. One would think that, given their exposure to public life, these church bodies would be familiar to everyone. They are all in the "Churches and Denominations" sections of the Yellow Pages in phone books across America. One passes signs announcing their presence at the highway entrance to smaller cities, or lets the eye scan announcements of their services in the suburban paper, or visually sweeps cityscapes where their towers mark the heights and horizons. Yet they remain strangely unfamiliar. I have been studying American church bodies professionally for a third of a century, yet I found any number of items about churches in this book that were new to me. More important, I found things I have known now ready to make themselves better known because they are patiently and faithfully expounded. I expect those who do not study churches professionally will find at least as much that is new, or newly stated, as did I. And they will find their interest sustained, their minds better stocked and stored, and, quite likely, their motives for actions in respect to others improved.

If one advertises all these benefits, some questions naturally arise. The first one is: if the denominations are such big deals, why has information such as that contained herein not been readily available? One way to answer is that some aspects of this information have been available. Arthur Carl Piepkorn's *Profiles in Belief* is a multi-volume work of encyclopedic proportions. But in strange ways it tells more than the NCC member churches need to know to get started on this subject, and the account of these churches is set in the context of a bewildering web of elements which are not the subject of present curiosity. And there are workhorse books like Frank S. Mead's *Handbook of Denominations*, which calls attention to the importance of this subject merely by its survival through many editions. Yet Mead achieves its purpose by being a necessarily prosaic, evened-out setting forth of the barebones aspects of these and many other churches.

The importance and charm of the Shriver work before you is its organization of the information one needs for "getting to know you" purposes among churches that already have much to do with each other and are committed to having more to do. There are no wasted pages and few wasted words in such a work. When one needs to know around the National Football League it is confusing or irrelevant to scatter and thus bury the information by locking it into a sequence that randomly includes Brazilian soccer and Irish rugby teams. The NFL folk have certain kinds of things to do with each other that makes separated-out knowledge more urgent.

After discerning the makeup, the goal, and the genre of this book about denominations there comes time to ask questions not about a handbook to them, but about their existence and roles in the first place. What place does the denomination play in the context of American church life or, indeed, American life as a whole? Most of us who write about the past and the present in American religion do not organize our books around denominations, the way our predecessors did one hundred years ago. Today the books have to do with themes: the roles of women in religion; the rise of health care in churchly settings; the relation of religion to industrialization or nationalism; the webbing of religion and politics.

One hundred years ago the denominations played a different role than they do now; that they have changed is in no small part

the result of the National Council of Churches and its predecessor, the Federal Council of Churches, and the many state and
local councils that are their kin closer to home. The ecumenical
era and spirit conspired to make the denominations not less relevant but relevant in different ways than before. A century ago
one needed maps of the sort this book presents for defensive purposes. The denominations were not in shooting wars, but they
were in competition and often represented enemy territory. Certainly denominations that were solidly white had nothing to do
with and probably disdained or feared those churches made up
of Blacks. To Protestants the Orthodox were remote, bearded,
"icon-kissers," idolaters of a sort. Methodists vied with Baptists
on the frontier, and both ganged up on the Disciples of Christ.
One was curious about others the way people need reconnais-
sance maps concerning enemy territory or home bases of spies.

Today it is hard to revisit the folklore of the frontier cir-
cuit riders, the accounts of bravado or peevishness among com-
petitive church builders, or expressions of ignorance about the
fellow-Christian that often characterized pre-ecumenical life in
America. One way to conjure it would be to listen to the ways
Fundamentalists talk about the churches in this book; they are
ignorant of their purposes and suspicious of their intentions.
So they speak out of ignorance or they deliberately misrepre-
sent them. Since this is a book about Christians, its author and
introducers also have to be honest and humble enough to say
that many members of the churches belonging to the National
Council in turn speak with mixtures of ignorance and hostil-
ity when they deal with aggressive Fundamentalists, whom they
fear.

The churches in this handbook do not fear each other, or at
least their fears do not follow denominational boundaries. So
the negative reasons for being familiar with each other have dis-
appeared. That leaves the positive ones, and this book is entirely
positive. To speak in such cheerful terms still does not address
the issue of denominations and their new kinds of importance.

The old importances have diminished or been compromised.
One could sound a bit ironic or cynical and say that if once one
needed accounts of other churches in order to know who was

figuratively shooting at you, or at whom you should shoot — as denominations accused each other of false doctrine, false consciousness, fake piety, foolish practices — today one needs them to understand their *internal* tensions. In recent decades we have seen Southern Baptist fight Southern Baptist, Missouri Lutheran fight Missouri Lutheran, and the like. And there are tensions, duly accounted for, in any number of the ecumenically-minded churches mentioned here. But while denominations, like families, may have conflict, they do not exist in order to fight. So the denominations have vastly nobler purposes than to serve as arenas of conflict.

Peggy L. Shriver gives many clues concerning the roles and importance of denominational existence. There is, each time, at least a small section on "Major Doctrines." Once upon a time doctrines would have taken up all the space, not because people lived by or for these doctrines, pure and simple, but because theologians and historians acted as if they did. The doctrines have been and in their own way remain significant. In many of the bodies discussed here — I would only get in trouble if I mentioned so many as one of them — doctrine, dogma, tenets, beliefs, ideas, are of first importance. The leaders would say that if these doctrines go, the churches which held them should go. For the most part, however, we need to see how these churches located doctrine alongside modes of organization, within the stages of their histories, and in the context of their actions.

What one has in the denominations of today are groups which are dysfunctional for older purposes; I have cited their dysfunctionality as staging points for fighting each other and implied that the "major doctrines" do not always match the boundaries of denominations in an ecumenical age. But if they malfunction in some respects and are dysfunctional in others, they have many functions, and these we need to know.

The picture of the family used above for comparison might serve now for description. Families have traditions, and they nurture these at reunions, in scrapbooks, around the dinner table. Denominations have traditions, and they encourage regard for them in conventions, at rites and ceremonies, in the literature they produce, when they come together to worship. Families do not "write everything down," do not always live by rules and regulations. They live by their histories, their stories, their inherited patterns of action, the innovations of their young, their experience of change. Denominations do that, too, and this book presents a highly condensed digest version of what the things are by which they live. Some of these churches are considered liberal; this book shows that liberal churches have traditions as rich as those which define themselves as traditionalist. Denominations have practical functions. If some Americans dismiss organized religion for the "privatized," "pick and choose," "a la carte" versions of belief, they dribble off into inconsequence in the face of common actions by social forces which serve across the generations. They have little to pass on to new generations, nothing with which to confront the present one, no basis for effecting change.

Church bodies, on the other hand, however undramatic and prosaic many of their activities, exist to further certain purposes. Their thousands of local manifestations, their congregations and parishes, may not always yield all or even most of their powers, rights and sympathies to their denominations in convention or to "headquarters." Yet they are mutually engaged, involved with each other, responsive to their elected and appointed leadership just as that leadership, over the long pull, is responsive to what goes on in the local entities.

When these congregations wish to provide a professional ministry for themselves and others in the next generation, they support theological schools. They want these schools to be expressive at least in broad outline of the "major doctrines," the "worship," the "organization" — I am peeking at the Shriverian subheadings in these chapters — of the denominations of which they are a part. They wish to send workers to relate to Christians of their kin and kind in other nations, the poor world, the Third World? They may possibly work through inventions called "parachurches," but odds are they will work through these denominations and their agents. They publish, they provide programs, they plan, they meet with others in "ecumenical involvements" through these denominations.

Here, then, is a map of these church bodies and a beginning of a guide through the mazeways they represent. By clustering churches in the light of their origins and provenance ("European/Asian, American"), their ethnic or racial makeup ("African-American"), their doctrinal tradition ("Orthodox"), or their distinguishing characteristic ("Peace"), author Shriver has been helpful. Here is not a simple alphabetized soup of denominations but a charted set of churches each of which fill certain niches and pursue decisive roles.

To speak of origins, race, doctrine, or characteristics as being dominant may sound as if this book reinforces old notions attacked by Paul in First Corinthians. Their Christ seems divided; some seem to be of Paul, some of Cephas. Where is their oneness in Christ? One might answer to that question that their mere presence here as committed members of an ecumenical organization suggests that they have determined to respond to the call of the Holy Spirit. This means that they wish ever more to realize their oneness in Christ.

Whether or not this Council or other agencies or new actions bring about visible realizations of such oneness is a question left to the future, to God. For now it is important to know the families which make up the extended family of faith in America; the subcommunities which help make up the Great Community called the Christian Church. Any book which helps members become familiar with the company they keep and the gifts this company bring deserves a welcome these days, so welcome to this one, titled *Having Gifts that Differ*.

MARTIN E. MARTY
The University of Chicago

1

CHURCHES OF
EUROPEAN/ASIAN ORIGIN

THE EPISCOPAL CHURCH

By action of its 1967 General Convention "The Episcopal Church" has been an alternative legal name for "The Protestant Episcopal Church in the United States of America," a title legal since 1789. The long prior debate over the appropriateness of the word "Protestant" in its name points to a significant self-perception of this province of the worldwide Anglican Communion. Frenchman Jerome Cornelis sums up this perception: "Emerging from the Reformation but feeling itself to be in continuity with the ancient Church, the Anglican Communion being both Catholic and evangelical has always considered itself as a bride-church committed to the reconciliation of the catholic-type and protestant-type communities."

Historically, the Church of England became an entity separate from the Roman Catholic Church in 1534 with the declaration of royal supremacy by King Henry VIII and his parliament after a dispute over the king's right to divorce Catherine of Aragon. Subsequent steps, especially those of Queen Elizabeth, called the Elizabethan Settlement, revealed a segment of the church eager for reform, for new church-state relationships, and for access to Scripture (through Tyndale's translation, and then the King James Version).

Anglicanism first took root on American shores in Virginia, followed soon by Maryland. Other early church congregations were St. Philip's in Charleston (1682), King's Chapel in

11

Boston (1689), Christ Church in Philadelphia (1695), and Trinity Church in New York (1697). In the Puritan stronghold of Massachusetts and other parts of New England, Anglicanism faced a struggle, as it did in New York with the Dutch, until New York was finally captured by the English in 1674. England's Society for the Propagation of the Gospel in Foreign Parts sent missionaries to the colonies, some three hundred up to the Revolution, after which all S.P.G. support was withdrawn. The Revolutionary War caused anguish for many Anglicans, who had taken an oath of loyalty to their English king. As many as 70,000 loyalists may have left the country for the Canadian maritime provinces and the West Indies. The church also suffered from an apathetic response in England to an urgent request for bishops. Despite these problems, a constitutional framework was completed in 1789 for the separate Protestant Episcopal Church in the U.S.A. Samuel Seabury, the first Anglican bishop consecrated to minister outside the British Isles, and three other bishops, two consecrated at Lambeth, joined to consecrate the first Episcopal bishop on national soil, Thomas John Claggett of Maryland.

The new Protestant Episcopal Church was influenced by the democratic spirit of the young nation, and the role of laity distinguished it from the Church of England, as also did its complete separation from state control. Although it enjoyed a season of revival, it did not get caught up in either of the "Great Awakenings." The church did expand with the nation, however, and has had a long history of mission among Native Americans, notably the Oneida Indians in New York and later in Wisconsin, to which the Oneidas were deported. Though not matching some other Protestant bodies in evangelical expansion, their growth was still remarkable in the early 1800s. For example, between 1833 and 1853 the number of communicants tripled, doubling again between 1860 and 1870.

Although the Revolutionary War was disastrous for Episcopalians, the Civil War proved them to be resilient, so that only during the Civil War itself was there a separate organization of the Protestant Episcopal Church in the Confederate States of America. In 1865 the northern presiding bishop's invitation to the southern bishops to attend the General Convention was accepted by some, and in a few months the southern church renewed its affiliation. The Episcopal Church participated in the early twentieth-century missionary expansion, with particular attention to China, Japan, Central and South America, and the Philippines. It also became vigorously involved in the Social Gospel movement, being one of the first communions to establish a national commission on social problems with paid staff.

Recent decades have seen the Episcopal Church struggle to make good its claim, in the words of Presiding Bishop Edmond Lee Browning, that "this church of ours is open to all — there shall be no outcasts." It has striven to work on the issues of racism, with special programs and grants to racial and ethnic minorities, special committees and commissions on Indian Work, Hispanic Affairs, and an Appalachian People's Service Organization. It has weathered a storm of controversy over revision of its cherished *Book of Common Prayer* and the ordination of women. Increased attention to education and other efforts at renewal, such as the Cursillo movement, have sought to address a troubling membership decline, a membership which peaked in 1966 with 3,647,297 members. The Episcopal Church engages in several ecumenical dialogues while being a constituent member of the Anglican Communion, in communion with the See of Canterbury.

Major Doctrines
"One canon...two testaments, three creeds, four general councils, five centuries and the series of Fathers in that period...determine the boundary of our faith," declared Lancelot Andrewes, a seventeenth-century Bishop of Winchester and a translator of the Bible. Continuity with the early church, an economy of essential doctrine or fundamentals necessary for salvation, and the constant appeal to Scripture describe the doctrinal stance of the Anglican tradition. Beyond this, Anglicans do not claim unique doctrinal distinction. Considering themselves to be continuous with the *Ecclesia Anglicana* of ancient times, yet influenced both by Lutheranism on the Continent and evan-

gelicalism in its own reforming ranks, Anglicans are committed, said Archbishop Ramsey, "not to a vague position wherein the Evangelical and the Catholic views are alternatives, but to the Scriptural faith wherein both elements are one." In the Reformation period a set of Articles of Religion, gradually refined to Thirty-Nine Articles, was adopted in 1572 and taken in the American Church into the Prayer Book in 1792. But the heart of Episcopalianism is the *Book of Common Prayer* itself, its noble liturgy a magnificent gathering and adaptation of rich liturgical tradition by Archbishop Cranmer and his associates in 1549, and revised in succeeding centuries.

Geography

Baptized membership in 1986 figures was 2,504,507. An illuminating 1984 *State of the Church* report by Rev. John Schultz documents that between 1966 and 1984 some 120,000 adults were baptized, 93,000 adults baptized elsewhere were confirmed, and 82,000 new members were received from other branches of the catholic church. He says, "This infusion of new blood has changed the make-up of our constituency so that now nearly sixty percent of our membership was not raised in the Episcopal Church, but came to us by choice as adults." In the latter part of that period there were defections from the Episcopal Church to form five separate bodies, the largest of which is the Anglican Catholic Church, organized in 1978 and claiming 6,500 members.

Organization

"The effective unit of government is the diocese," says historian J. W. C. Wand, where the bishop, surrounded by presbyters, is responsible for governance of "home affairs" and also acts as "liaison officer" with other dioceses. Each diocese is part of a province, which is part of a regional or national church, and each regional or national church is part of the Anglican Communion, whose bishops meet every ten years at the Lambeth Conference. At work in over eighty countries, the Anglican Communion's membership worships in one hundred and seventy languages. The first Lambeth Conference in 1867 had only seventy-six bishops, while in 1988 some 1,200 bishops and others gathered at Canterbury. By the turn of the century it is anticipated that the majority of Anglicans will live in Africa, Asia and Latin America. Each national or regional church has its primate, archbishop, or presiding bishop, and is in full communion with the Church of England, and in particular with the Archbishop of Canterbury, Primate of all England. An Anglican Consultative Council meets every other year. Regular Primates' meetings are also called. There are three traditional orders of ordained ministry: deacon, priest and bishop. In the Episcopal Church in the U.S.A., a General Convention is composed of a House of Bishops and a House of Deputies (each diocese represented with four clergy, four lay). In 1970 the constitution was changed to allow women to serve in the House of Deputies, most local parish vestries already permitting women's participation. Women were allowed to be deacons also in 1970 and ordained as priests in 1976, a matter of continuing debate and emotional trauma throughout Anglicanism.

Worship
Both worship and doctrine, indeed the very core of the Episcopal Church, are encompassed in the *Book of Common Prayer.* It has been revised in its American form several times, but the most recent revision, given approval in 1979, stirred heated debate. Churches in the Anglican tradition vary in the degree to which they are "high" or "low" church, the "high church" tending toward what some call "Anglo-Catholic." The Prayer Book contains liturgies of morning and evening prayer, the Eucharist, special liturgies for holy days, for marriage, burial, confirmation, Baptism, and a section of historical documents of the church. It cannot be overstressed that it embodies the essence of Anglicanism. In 1988 Barbara C. Harris was elected the first woman bishop.

Ecumenical Involvement
True to its sense of special ecumenical responsibility, the Episcopal Church has been a founding member of National and World Councils of Churches, the Consultation on Church

Union, and other ecumenical endeavors. In 1886 the House of Bishops at the General Convention meeting in Chicago adopted a Declaration concerning unity stimulated by William Reed Huntington. The 1888 Lambeth Conference took his four essential elements that supply a basis for the unity of the church, now called the "Chicago-Lambeth Quadrilateral," and issued an appeal for reunion. In brief, these are the Bible ("rule and ultimate standard of faith"), the Nicene Creed and/or Apostles' Creed as baptismal confession, the sacraments of Baptism and Holy Communion, and "the Historic Episcopate, locally adapted in the methods of its administration" — the element causing the most controversy.

A National Ecumenical Consultation was held in September 1987 in Chicago to recognize the centenary of the Chicago-Lambeth Quadrilateral, to which members of ecumenical dialogues and other ecumenical guests were invited. In recent years the Episcopal Church has engaged in extensive dialogues with several major church traditions, such as the Orthodox, Lutheran, Reformed, and Roman Catholic. These dialogues include ARCIC (the Anglican Roman Catholic International Consultation). The centenary in Chicago heard the presiding bishop call for interdependence of these dialogues and local participation in them, as well as the need to pursue together dialogues with people of other living religions. It also listened to candid assessments of Episcopal ecumenism by other ecumenical leaders, both words of criticism and hope.

EVANGELICAL LUTHERAN CHURCH IN AMERICA

Like a braid of three strands that themselves are composed of many threads, the Evangelical Lutheran Church in America weaves together a remarkable number of separate church histories. The powerful religious impact of Martin Luther, which spread throughout Europe, reached the United States through many national groups intent upon establishing in the new land their own distinct Lutheran vision of Christian faith and practice.

One of those strands, the American Lutheran Church, contains a thread that, when followed, leads one back to a farmer who experienced a complete change of heart while singing and working in a Norwegian field in April 1796. Farmer Hans Nielson Hauge became the leader of a group of devout moralists and reformer critics of the state church — the Haugeans, one of whom founded a rigorous church in the U.S. It became a forerunner of "Hauge's Synod" and the Norwegian Lutheran Church in America. Four German-American Synods in Ohio, Iowa, Buffalo and Texas formed the "old" ALC of 1930 after reaching a hard-fought compromise over "inerrancy" of Scripture. This German group, the Haugeans and other Norwegian groups, and a Danish-background body, the United Evangelical Lutheran Church, became the American Lutheran Church in 1960. The Lutheran Free Church joined three years later.

A second strand of the "braid" of the 1987 ELCA union, the Lutheran Church in America, also contains many threads, with German, Swedish (Augustana), Finnish (Suomi Synod), and Danish heritage. The remarkable philosopher Søren Kierkegaard and pastor-hymnwriter Nikolai Grundtvig are nineteenth-century Danes who affected Lutheranism in America. Grundtvig's spiritual heirs brought Danish culture to the U.S. and were known for their buoyant faithfulness as "happy Danes." Another group of Danes, called "holy" or "sad Danes," brought an earnest, moral vigor to the U.S. churches they founded. Some of both groups ended up in both the ALC and the LCA. The United Lutheran Church in America (German), founded in 1918 from three groups of the Muhlenberg tradition, became the leader in a merger with the three smaller Swedish, Finnish, and Danish churches to form the Lutheran Church in America. The ULCA brought to the LCA an ecumenical, catholic spirit as the LCA became constituted in Detroit in 1962 under the leadership of Franklin Clark Fry, who also served for fourteen years as chair of the World Council of Churches central committee until his death in 1968.

The third, smaller strand of the ELCA braid is the Association of Evangelical Lutheran Churches, which never did constitute itself as a denomination. The AELC represents much of the leading talent in arts, theology, education and ministry as well as 275 congregations drawn from the Lutheran Church–Missouri Synod. Known for its strict confessionalism in doctrine and practice, the LC-MS was gradually opening doors to broader understanding through the efforts of Concordia Seminary in St. Louis. Teachers like Arthur Carl Piepkorn and Richard Caemmerer confronted the church with fresh and vital insights of Lutheranism.

But Concordia's leadership toward broader Lutheran relationships was challenged when J. A. O. Preus became president of LC-MS. When Concordia's president was suspended in 1974, the students voted a moratorium on classes and 80 percent of the faculty joined them to form Concordia Seminary-in-Exile, or Seminex. Meanwhile, moderates of LC-MS had formed a network called Evangelical Lutherans in Mission, which became the AELC, an "interim denomination" that was influential in initiating union talks with the LCA and ALC. Some 5.3 million Lutherans are now gathered in the ELCA, which was constituted April 30, 1987. In Chicago an ecumenical assemblage of 3,000 people gathered to install Bishop Herbert W. Chilstrom as the first bishop of the new Evangelical Lutheran Church in America, fourth largest U.S. denomination. A gold ribbon was cut to open the churchwide offices in Chicago in January 1988, as the ELCA began to function officially.

About 63 percent of all Lutherans are members of the ELCA, 31 percent of the LC-MS, 5 percent of the Wisconsin Evangelical Lutheran Synod, and 1 percent of some seventeen other remaining Lutheran churches. There are more than 18,500 Lutheran congregations in the United States. A small group opposed to the ELCA union formed the American Association of Lutheran Churches, some others of them going to the Association of Free Lutheran Congregations, which was established twenty-five years ago.

Major Doctrines

The ELCA constitution Confession of Faith is trinitarian and accepts the Apostles', Nicene, and Athanasian Creeds and the Unaltered Augsburg Confession. It accepts other confessional writings in the Book of Concord as further valid interpretations. The canonical Scriptures are the "inspired Word of God and the authoritative source and norm of its proclamation, faith, and life," and the Gospel is "the power of God to create and sustain the Church for God's mission in the world" and "the power of God for the salvation of all who believe."

Geography

The beginning membership of the ELCA was 5,307,285, and its congregations are located in every state in the U.S.A., in Puerto Rico, and in the Virgin Islands. It has single congregations in the Bahamas, Bermuda, Denmark, Norway, and Canada. The largest number of congregations is in the North Central and Middle Atlantic regions of the U.S.

Organization

Congregations relate to one of sixty-five geographic Synods, which are grouped into nine regional centers of mission, to foster interdependent relationships among the churchwide organization, the Synods, and the congregations. A common Confession of Faith and common Statement of Purpose are required parts of congregational, synodical, and churchwide constitutions.

The Synod provides pastoral care for congregations, ordained ministers, and associates in ministry within its geographic area. Synods develops mission resources and do outreach along with congregations and the national structure. The ELCA enters into relationships with governmental, ecumenical, and societal agencies and develops churchwide policies in consultation with Synods and congregations.

Each Synod has a bishop, and there is one bishop churchwide. Each interdependent part has its own legislative assembly — congregational voters' meetings, synodical assemblies at least once every two years, and a churchwide assembly held biennially. The first regular assembly of the ELCA was set for 1989. There are four churchwide officers: a bishop, a vice president, a secretary, and a treasurer. The bishop must be ordained, the vice president must be lay, the secretary and the treasurer may be either. The ELCA named a woman, Christine Grumm, to be its first vice president. All three uniting bodies in the ELCA had voted by 1976 to ordain women.

Although Lutherans are predominantly northern European, the American churches are striving to reach out toward Blacks, Hispanics, Native Americans and other minority groups in the U.S.

Worship

The ELCA affirms that worship is central in the lives of its members as they participate in God's mission in the world. The Triune God is worshipped in the proclamation of the Word and the administration of the sacraments (Holy Baptism and Holy Communion) and through lives of prayer, praise, thanksgiving, witness, and service. Sacraments are the sign and seal of God's grace to the individual. Baptism is a "saving bath, a washing of regeneration," and faith is required to receive the blessings but not to make Baptism efficacious. Like Baptism, the Lord's Supper is "wholesome and salutary medicine" to bestow life upon body and soul, an anticipation of one's own resurrection. Lutheran doctrine speaks of the mystery of the Real Presence of Christ in the bread and wine. There is no official order for worship services in the ELCA. The most commonly used resource for worship, however, is the *Lutheran Book of Worship*, published in 1978. It includes liturgies, hymns, lectionaries, and prayers. The Lutheran service is designed, says F. E. Mayer, "to offer the reconciled Christian an opportunity to bring (his) eucharistic sacrifice in the chants and hymns, in the prayers, in (his) witness and even in the celebration of the Holy Eucharist."

Ecumenical Involvement

The ELCA is a member of the Lutheran World Federation, the World Council of Churches, and the National Council of Churches of Christ in the U.S.A., but its Constituting Convention directed that continued membership in the WCC and the NCC should be studied and given further consideration at the regular churchwide assembly in 1989. At the time of uniting, the American Lutheran Church was a member of the WCC but not the NCC, while the Lutheran Church in America was a member of both and the Association of Evangelical Lutheran Churches was a member of neither. Many Synods are members of state councils of churches. The ELCA has specific mutual relationships with the Evangelical Lutheran Church in Canada, the Lutheran Church–Missouri Synod, and the Episcopal Church. It is conducting theological conversations with the Presbyterian Church (U.S.A.), the Reformed Church in America, and the United Church of Christ. It participates in bilateral dialogue with the Episcopal Church, the Orthodox churches, and the Roman Catholic Church. Dialogues have been completed with the Baptists and the United Methodist Church.

Lutherans have a strong sense of worldwide relationship

through the Lutheran World Federation headquartered in Geneva in the same building as the World Council of Churches. It is a powerful symbol of their desire to cultivate a confessional identity amid an increasing awareness of the wider unity of the church already given oneness in Christ.

HUNGARIAN REFORMED CHURCH IN AMERICA

People from other nations often marvel at the number of denominations or communions that exist side-by-side in the United States of America. Although many of these groups are home grown in fertile individualistic American soil, others represent the difficult struggle of immigrants to participate and assimilate or maintain their special identity in American life. The Hungarian Reformed Church in America is a classic illustration of this struggle.

Hungarians came to the United States sporadically in the early years of American society. The high point of Hungarian immigration preceded World War I, but even then about 70 percent of those who came to the U.S. returned again to their homeland in Hungary. The Reformation movement had received a response in many of the countries of Europe, causing Reformed churches to be organized in Germany, France, Holland, and Hungary among others. When immigrants from these countries found reformers in the U.S., many of them simply banded together, so that the first organized Hungarian Reformed congregations affiliated under the aegis of the (German) Reformed Church in the United States (RCUS) in 1890, both in Pittsburgh and Cleveland. Other Hungarian immigrant congregations established relationships with the Presbyterian Church in the U.S.A.

In 1904 six Hungarian congregations that had previously affiliated with the RCUS decided in New York City to form their own classis, along with some newly formed churches they had organized, and to place themselves under the care of the Reformed Church in Hungary. They received ministers and some aid from the mother church in Hungary. During this time of heavy immigration, a second classis had to be established. World War I broke contact with Hungary, and these American classes sought once again an American affiliation. Although the mother Hungarian church commended them to the Presbyterian Church in the U.S.A., the Presbyterians were reluctant to let them continue as ethnically-organized classes, so they made an agreement with the RCUS, which was willing to leave them intact. Under the "Tiffin (Ohio) Agreement," they and the Hungarian congregations that had not separated from the RCUS back in 1904 became four classes within the RCUS.

When the RCUS and Evangelical Synod merged in 1934 to form the Evangelical and Reformed Church, the Hungarians became the Magyar Synod (changed to Calvin Synod in 1964). The Evangelical and Reformed Church and Congregationalists later came together to form the United Church of Christ, and there is still a strong strain of Hungarians in the UCC–Calvin Synod.

But three Hungarian congregations were unhappy with the Tiffin Agreement and withdrew from the RCUS in 1921 (before either the E and R or UCC were established). Independent for three years, these congregations began to seek out one another and on December 9, 1924, they and four newly organized congregations formed a new denomination at Duquesne, Pennsylvania. It was called the Free Magyar Reformed Church in America until 1958, when they adopted the name Hungarian Reformed Church in America (HRCA).

During the past thirty-five years there have been three additional waves of immigration that have enriched the Hungarian Reformed Church in America: (1) the so-called Displaced Persons of the early 1950s; (2) the refugees of the October 23, 1956, uprising in Hungary; and (3) the great number of Hungarian Reformed refugees coming from Transylvania, Romania. The Reverend Gabor Csardas, a member of the delegation to the NCC Governing Board, testifies that the Presbyterians did "a tremendous job in resettling these refugees in this country and in our churches." Relationships with the Reformed Church in Hungary have improved in recent years. The typical "emigrant" mentality has changed into a mutual, although at times critical, understanding. However, the situation of the ethnic Hungarian Reformed churches in pre-war Hungary is of grave concern to the HRCA, first of all in Transylvania, where the church suffers oppression by the Romanian communist government, and secondly in Czechoslovakia (i.e., Slovakia), where the church is also under severe political pressure, particularly after the recent death of their bishop, Zsigmond Horvath. The HRCA renders assistance by providing some financial aid and exposing human rights violations. Ethnic Hungarian Reformed people in Yugoslavia and the Carpatho-Ukraine are in a much more acceptable position. Financial assistance is also rendered by the HRCA to ethnic Hungarian Reformed congregations in South America, Australia, and Western Europe.

Church historian Arthur C. Piepkorn says, "While emphasizing its distinctive European heritage, this church body has assimilated itself to the American scene." The church developed a mission program that initiated new congregations in various parts of the United States.

Major Doctrines

The Hungarian (Free Magyar) Reformed Church emphasizes its confessional heritage as essential to the Hungarian Reformed tradition, which is strongly Calvinistic. One objection raised to the Tiffin Agreement was doctrinal — although the RCUS had the Heidelberg Catechism as a doctrinal basis, it did not have the Second Helvetic Confession, both of which are symbolic books for the Reformed Hungarians. At the Synod of Debrecen in 1567 the Second Helvetic Confession was adopted as the basic doctrine of the church. The date 1567 is considered the establishment year of the Reformed Church in Hungary. The Second Helvetica and the Heidelberg Catechism have ever since been the twin symbolic books of the Reformed Church in Hungary and have been made the doctrinal standard of the HRCA. It is so stated in the church's constitution and it is part of the ordination vows of every minister. The voluntary church membership principle is also an important emphasis of the Hungarian Reformed Church in America.

Geography

The present Hungarian Reformed Church in America is made up of three classes — New York, Eastern and Western. There are congregations in New York, New Jersey, Pennsylvania, Ohio, Michigan, Florida, Arizona, Texas, California, the District of Columbia, and Ontario, Canada. The three classes constitute the Synod, with altogether thirty chartered congregations (one more being in the process of formation). Total membership has been reported as 10,500.

Most of the congregations are bilingual; a few have only Hungarian language services, while two have only English. In the bilingual congregations the English-speaking section is larger; in some the ratio on Sundays is 80 percent to 20 percent. There are practically no Black or Hispanic members; the few are spouses in racially mixed marriages. Approximately 25 percent are of non-Magyar background; these again are spouses in mixed marriages.

Organization

The HRCA has been governed by bishops (also called superintendents) from the very beginning. Although the church had protectors and benefactors from among the Hungarian aristocracy, the general participation of lay members in decision making (church councils) began only in the seventeenth century and became strong only in the eighteenth, when the church needed influential advocates at the Habsburg court. Still, the spiritual and doctrinal leadership remained in the hands of the clergy, headed by the bishops and greatly influenced by the theological schools (Sarospatak and Debrecen). The church's polity gradually developed into a system of dual leadership on all levels: each congregation has a pastor and a lay "curator" (chief elder); so does the seniorate (classis) have a senior (dean) and curator, and the church district has the bishop and district-curator, co-chairs of the respective judicatories. This system adopted by the HRCA is called by John T. McNeill, in *The History and Character of Calvinism*, a "constitutional episcopate." The bishop (called "arch-dean" until 1957) is the spiritual leader and chief administrator yet without "episcopal jurisdiction." He is elected for a stated term, at present four years. The Synod meets every two years; a Bishop's Council when necessary takes care of interim business. The classes meet annually. Individual churches have control over their own properties with certain restrictions by the higher judicatories. Assimilation to the American scene, as mentioned by Piepkorn, appears in the voluntary church membership principle instead of the old country parish system. Similarly, the congregations are self-supporting through voluntary contributions instead of the old country system of church taxation. (The "old country systems" referred to are the pre-World War II systems.)

The HRCA has no theological seminary. Many of its ministers had been trained in Hungary; a number of refugee ministers have arrived lately from Transylvania, others had come following the 1956 uprising, still others in the late forties and a few before that. If possible, ministerial candidates are sent to the Reformed Church in America seminary in New Brunswick or to the Presbyterian seminary in Princeton. A Board of Examination decides ministerial eligibility, based upon completion of the usual Master of Divinity degree as well as study of distinctive Hungarian church history and its two symbolic books. The shortage in bilingual ministers is becoming acute. The Board of Examination has authority to commission lay preachers. Women may be ordained as ministers or commissioned as lay preachers.

Worship

In Magyar-language services the church uses the worshipbook of the Reformed Church in Hungary of 1930. The new worshipbook published by the Reformed Church in Hungary in 1985 is known but not widely used. In English-language services, a translation of the Hungarian-language texts is used. Several translations of the Magyar liturgical texts exist; there is no single official English-language worshipbook. In congregational singing the Psalms are favored in both languages.

Certain features of the Magyar liturgy are being maintained in both languages: in the Communion liturgy, after the confession of sin and the Apostles' Creed, "public confession and vows" precedes the Declaration of Pardon; at baptisms, the promise of parents and godparents to instruct the child for future confirmation; in marriage vows, an oath of fidelity made by both partners but not to each other; and at funerals, the committal service at the grave consisting of readings from 1 Corinthians 15 followed by the Apostles' Creed.

The Communion service, although immediately following the worship of the Word, is a separate unit. There are, as a rule, six Communion services in the year: Lent, Easter, Pentecost, Thanksgiving for the New Bread (in July), Thanksgiving for the New Wine (in November), and Christmas. World Wide Communion has been added in some churches. In a few, monthly Communion services are observed. It is a rule that all types of services — Baptism, confirmation, wedding, funeral — should contain a sermon or homily. Sermons are expected to be strongly biblical.

Ecumenical Involvement

The HRCA is a member of the World Alliance of Reformed Churches, the National Council of Churches of Christ in the U.S.A., and the World Council of Churches. Through one of its delegates, the HRCA actively participates in the Roman Catholic–Presbyterian/Reformed Consultation (co-chairing for sixteen years) and in the Theological Committee of the Caribbean and North American Area Council of the World Alliance (secretary for over twelve years). It endeavors to be faithful to its over four-century-old Hungarian Reformed heritage as well as to John Calvin's legacy and the Swiss Reformation. At the same time, in partnership with other churches, it seeks to be part of the one church under a sovereign Lord.

KOREAN PRESBYTERIAN CHURCH IN AMERICA

The story of this rapidly growing new church in the United States logically begins in Korea. Protestant missionaries from the United States to Korea came from a number of denominations, but one direct ancestor of the Korean Presbyterian Church in America must surely be Dr. Samuel A. Moffett, a Presbyterian who arrived in Pyengyang, North Korea, in 1890 as the first resident Protestant missionary in North Korea. He began theological instruction for a few lay preachers and graduated his first class of seven men in 1907, when the first Korean Presbytery was also organized. The Presbytery included missionary representatives from four Presbyterian denominations — U.S. north and south, Canada, and Australia. One of the seven men ordained by this new Presbytery was a man who had stoned Dr. Moffett sixteen years earlier in the tough streets of Pyengyang.

During the years of Japanese occupation beginning with the second Sino-Japanese War of 1937–1945, many Christians suffered torture, imprisonment or death when they refused to acknowledge the Japanese emperor as a god. When the Japanese were defeated in World War II, the Russians overwhelmed North Korea and Christians were again a target for oppression and destruction. Many fled to the South, where the churches now thrive and yearn for news of relatives and friends in the North. Christianity flourishes in South Korea today, with some 20–25 percent of the population being Christian, compared to 3–4 percent throughout Asia. Of the 6.5 million Protestants (and 1.8 million Roman Catholics) in Korea, 4.3 million are Presbyterians. Churches are increasing in membership four times faster than the population is growing. The tiny seminary begun by Samuel Moffett is now located on the outskirts of Seoul and had an inclusive enrollment in 1987 of 2,300 students.

In recent years many Koreans have emigrated to the United States. Although many Korean Christians are Presbyterians when they arrive in the U.S., they feel the need of cultural sustenance from their home country, as did immigrants of many other ethnic churches founded in the U.S. Some Koreans have found their way into U.S. Presbyterian churches, now united in the Presbyterian Church (U.S.A.) But others have sought to maintain their separateness in culture and language, because they feel that the time is not yet right and comfortable for them to unite with American Presbyterians. Such congregations have gathered into churches like the Korean Presbyterian Church in America.

Ten years after the Korean Presbyterian Church in America began to organize in the United States it negotiated an agreement with the Presbyterian Church of Korea that recognized the independent existence of the KPCA. It is now a sister communion with the Presbyterian Church of Korea and also with the Korean Christian Church in Japan, both agreements being signed in 1986.

In Seoul, South Korea, there is a remarkable 60,000 member Young Nak Presbyterian Church. In the U.S. there is a Young Nak Presbyterian Church of Los Angeles, already with 4,000 members, that is building a $3.5 million complex on a $4.5 million site near Chinatown in Los Angeles. The KPCA, barely ten years old, is beginning to face the challenges of adapting to the influences of American democracy, to a larger role for women and laity in general, and to American cultural influence upon the church's second generation. In the spring of 1986 the KPCA General Assembly tried, but failed, to allow women elders, which is one example of beginning to respond to new cultural expectations.

Major Doctrines

Consistent with the Presbyterian heritage brought by missionaries to Korea, the KPCA Creed and Shorter Catechism printed in its constitution have a Reformed theology, Calvinist in its emphasis upon original sin of humankind, Christ's atonement to satisfy divine justice, predestination to salvation, and God's providential covenant of grace with human creatures. The theology is thoroughly trinitarian. Justified, adopted, sanctified believers are duty-bound to live according to the will of God, given in the Ten Commandments, and look toward redemption purchased by Christ and life eternal with God.

Geography

The KPCA has grown rapidly to almost 200 churches and 24,000 inclusive members, doubling in the past ten years. It has 225 ordained clergy with local charges; its three seminaries require a Master of Divinity degree. In the U.S. generally, as of 1987 there were 1,642 Christian churches composed of Korean Americans, of which 70 percent are considered Presbyterian. Of these 70 percent, 230 churches (with 33,465 members) are affiliated with the Presbyterian Church (U.S.A.). One-fourth of the KPCA membership is located in southern California. It is noteworthy that at least half of all Korean church members who have immigrated to the U.S. in the past twenty years were non-Christians when they arrived, but the percentage of church-going Koreans is higher in the U.S. now than in Korea. There are some 800,000 Koreans currently in the U.S.

Organization

Like other Presbyterian bodies, the KPCA is constituted with a Presbytery structure and a General Assembly. The Western Presbytery was formed in 1973, where more than half the Korean population of the U.S. resides, chiefly southern California. The Central Presbytery was organized in 1974, the Eastern in 1975, and Canada Presbytery in 1979. The Assembly, established in 1976, is the highest administrative authority and is composed of ministers and representing elders sent by each Presbytery. It has administrative oversight of the entire church and communicates with other denominations. In 1986 the moderator of the Presbyterian Church (U.S.A.) General Assembly, William H. Wilson, brought congratulatory greetings to the tenth Assembly of the KPCA, noting over a hundred years of mission partnership in Korea and expressing joy in the KPCA's decade of growth with anticipation of carrying out common mission in the future. Local churches have sessions composed of a pastor, associate pastor, and elders to administer and oversee the temporal and spiritual life of the congregation. The local general board meeting elects "elders, deacons, and female elders." A minimum of five pastors, five sessions and three hundred members are needed to organize a Presbytery.

Worship

Interpretation of Scripture in preaching is focal to Presbyterian worship. Baptism and the Lord's Supper are sacraments instituted by Christ, and Baptism is administered to those who confess faith in Christ and also to their children. The Lord's Supper is a remembrance of Christ's death, a sign of Christ's blessing through the Holy Spirit, and it should be administered until Christ's second coming. The KPCA upholds in its constitution the freedom of conscience, which is ruled solely by God. However, just as individuals have freedom of conscience, so a denomination or church has the freedom to establish its rules on methods and qualifications for membership.

Ecumenical Involvement

The Korean Presbyterian Church in America, in its eagerness to establish ecumenical relationships with the larger church, sought membership in the National Council of Churches in 1982, when it was only half the required size for membership. Its rapid growth led to a reapplication and a vote into membership in the National Council of Churches in November 1986.

THE MORAVIAN CHURCH IN AMERICA
(UNITAS FRATRUM)

In 1957 the Moravian Church celebrated its 500th anniversary, making it sixty years older than Luther's Reformation act of nailing ninety-five theses to the Wittenberg door. Moravia and Bohemia (now Czechoslovakia) were first converted to Christianity by Greek Orthodox missionaries and had their own translation of the Bible; thus the people resisted when they later fell under Roman Catholic jurisdiction. Prague philosophy professor John Hus led the people's protest that resulted in his being burned at the stake as a heretic by the Council of Constance in 1415.

After forty years of initial confusion and loss of leadership, a group called the "Unity of the Brethren," or *Unitas Fratrum* in Latin, was established in 1457. Soon it had published a hymnal and a Bohemian Bible, the Kralitz Bible, but during the struggles of the Counter-Reformation most of the group were compelled to give up their faith, leave the country, or be killed. John Amos Comenius, a great educator and bishop, led some of these new Protestants through the deep mountain snow into Poland in January 1628, where many were assimilated into Lutheran and Reformed communities of faith. For over a hundred years a "hidden seed" of faith survived, as Comenius had prayed it would, in an "underground church" in Bohemia and Moravia, until a convert to Pietism, Christian David, discovered that they

33

would be welcome and protected in freedom of faith by Count Nicholas von Zinzendorf, a young nobleman of Saxony. Unitas Fratrum refugees settled on Zinzendorf's estate and formed a community called Herrnhut, whose neighboring Germans called them "the Moravians," and this became acceptable usage over time. Zinzendorf became increasingly involved in the community, helping it draft "The Brotherly Agreement," which was adopted May 12, 1727. The Agreement was followed soon after by a Pentecost-type spiritual renewal on August 13 that found expression in missionary outreach. Concentrating on pioneer evangelism to peoples who had never heard the Gospel, the Moravians first established a mission to the slaves in the West Indies in 1732 and were among the earliest of Protestant missionaries.

Mission to Native American Indians brought the Moravians to Georgia in 1735, where they met and influenced John Wesley. Five years later they established a permanent settlement in Nazareth, Pennsylvania; evangelist George Whitefield had invited them there to help build an orphanage. Soon they had built their own community, and a congregation was organized in 1742 in Bethlehem. An offer from Lord Granville to sell a large tract of land in what is now North Carolina led them to establish a settlement (Wachovia) there, and the Southern Province of the Moravian Church at Bethabara (1753) and Salem (1771) was soon underway. Mission efforts among Native Americans continued into the 1800s. After 1850 Moravians did home mission work among German immigrants, especially in the U.S. Midwest and western Canada.

Major Doctrines
"In essentials, unity, in non-essentials, liberty, and in all things charity (or love)" summarizes the Moravian evangelical Protestant attitude toward doctrine, whose source is the Bible, "the only rule of our faith and life." No special Moravian Church creed has been developed, but a number of creeds, including the Apostles' Creed and the Nicene Creed, have gained special importance. The Unitas Fratrum maintains that "all creeds formulated by the Christian Church stand in need of con-

stant testing in the light of the Holy Scriptures," according to the General Synod of 1957's statement, "The Ground of the Unity."

Geography

The Northern Province of the Moravian Church in the U.S. has its headquarters in Bethlehem, Pennsylvania, and it extends to the West coast and into Canada. It is divided into three districts (Eastern, Western, Canadian), and has 110 churches with an inclusive membership of 32,180. The Southern Province, whose headquarters is Winston-Salem, North Carolina, has 56 churches and an inclusive membership of 21,722, some of whom are in Florida and Georgia. (The North-South division dates from colonial days.) The Moravian Church has congregations in twenty states or provinces of the U.S. and Canada. Extensive missions, especially the Caribbean basin and Africa, have church members that outnumber U.S. and European church membership by four to one. In Europe the Moravians operate not only as a separate denomination but as a service agency of the state church and receive support for their continuing foreign missions and societies.

Organization

Membership of the local church comprises a church council, which meets annually to conduct business and to elect its officers and delegates. Usually a local church has a Board of Elders for spiritual care and congregational oversight and a Board of Trustees for temporal business, such as budget and building maintenance. The Northern Province has District Conferences, to which the local churches send delegates and which in turn elects delegates to the Provincial Synod. The District Conferences have an elected District Executive Board, with one salaried executive head. The Northern and Southern Provinces each have a Provincial Elders' Conference, which is a general administrative board. The highest authority of the provinces is Provincial Synods, or legislative assemblies, which give executive authority to boards elected by the Synods. The form of government is usually described as "conferential." Although the Moravians have bishops, the office is an acknowledgement of spiritual stature and carries no administrative power or responsibility as it does in many other churches.

Worship

Moravian worship has stressed the element of joy, congregational singing, and in many places instrumental music, especially brass. Moravians were the leading composers of vocal and instrumental music in colonial and early American periods. Moravians stand between more liturgical traditions and freer worship, with considerable diversity among Moravian congregations. They observe two sacraments: Baptism and Communion. Because of their strong sense of community, they sometimes in jest call fellowship a third sacrament. Communion is generally celebrated about six times a year, with the service consisting primarily of congregational singing. The love feast, a simple fellowship meal (usually composed of coffee and a roll) within the context of worship, is a custom in most congregations. Infant Baptism is the normal practice, but believer's Baptism is not unknown.

Ecumenical Involvement

Moravians of both provinces are members of the World Council of Churches and the National Council of Churches. When the Unitas Fratrum remnant was gathered under his protection at Herrnhut, Count Zinzendorf saw them as providing spiritual vitality to the existing state church, as "a church within a church." Today in Europe the Moravians function in this way, but also as an independent church, as they have developed in the United States. Yet one of the essentials of Moravian doctrine is the oneness of believers in Christ Jesus. *The Moravian Covenant for Christian Living* recognizes "no distinction between those who are one in the Lord." It mandates Christ's commandment to "demonstrate by word and deed that we are one in Christ."

THE POLISH NATIONAL CATHOLIC CHURCH

Catholics from Poland came to the New World with no intention of breaking with their church, but, as persons with spirit, eagerness to get ahead, and devotion to their Polish heritage, they sought increased religious liberty in their new environment. Both the winsome freedom of American Protestants and their bigotry toward "papists" contributed to the eventual formation of the Polish National Catholic Church at the turn of the twentieth century. Observing the dignity of American Protestants, their sense of co-ownership of their churches and mutual respect between pastor and parishioner, many Polish Roman Catholic immigrants yearned for a larger administrative role in their own parishes. Protestant suspicion toward the large influx of Roman Catholics in the mid-nineteenth century nudged many Roman Catholics to espouse a strong Americanism to prove their loyalty. Irish and German priests and bishops in particular urged assimilation into American culture, which the Polish Catholics resisted.

This resistance had historical roots in Europe during the ninth century, when the Greek missionaries Cyril and Methodius brought Christianity to Slavonic peoples, using Scripture and liturgy in the Slavonic language, for which they were criticized and recalled by the Bishop of Rome. Attempts to establish the Reformation movement in Poland in the sixteenth and seventeenth centuries were also crushed. Rome eventually won the day. Some Poles, upset with both political and religious oppression, emigrated to the United States before the Civil War. Some came as soldiers with Generals Kosciuszko and Pulaski to fight the war for independence beside other American colonists. Economic necessity brought most to the United States in the post-Civil War era.

Priests were scarce in the U.S., so many Polish lay people organized and built parishes themselves with money that was also scarce. Occasional imposition of non-Polish priests, who took charge of the buildings, finances and affairs of the parish while discouraging preservation of cultural ethnicity, became deeply resented by Polish parishioners, especially in several large cities with heavy concentrations of Polish people. In other instances, insensitive Polish pastors ruled parishes with a heavy hand. In Chicago Rev. Anthony Kozlowski established an independent set of parishes and was consecrated bishop by Old Catholic bishops of Switzerland, Germany and Holland in 1847, and his "Polish Catholic Church" joined forces upon his death with a group forming in Scranton, Pennsylvania. Meanwhile, in Buffalo, New York, an independent parish, which became headquarters of another movement, was organized.

A mining and industrial center, Scranton was the persisting focus of the formation of a new church. Polish people, sometimes encouraged to settle by mine owners who wanted them to resist trade unions, became the "bottom rung of the social ladder," and they sensed this attitude even in their priest, Rev. Richard Aust. Appealing to the hierarchy and under near-riot conditions, they asked to have this unsympathetic priest expelled. In one incident their women stood as a barricade against the police at the door of the Sacred Hearts of Jesus and Mary Polish Catholic Church.

At issue were their administrative rights in the handling of church financial affairs and the selection of their own priest. A group of several hundred dissident families organized a new parish, St. Stanilaus Bishop and Martyr. They looked to Rev. Francis Hodur, who had been born of a peasant family in Poland

and had studied theology in Cracow. Hodur had come to the U.S. already a strong proponent of religious liberty. At their invitation he accepted the pastorate of the "independent" Catholic congregation in Scranton in 1897 and was excommunicated by the Roman Catholic Bishop of Scranton in 1898, despite a visit to Rome which he thought had been positive. During an evening talk on Savonarola on the day his excommunication was read aloud to the congregation, Hodur burned the notice. He later wrote, "What naive people the bishops are. They still think in terms of medieval times when at the beckon of a pope, the cardinals and bishops, the innocent hands of Hus and Savonarola were shackled. ... I have been excommunicated for you, my people, because I have loved you too much. ... "

In 1907, three years after his election by a Synod, Hodur went to Utrecht and was consecrated a bishop in the Old Catholic Cathedral of St. Gertrude, which gave him apostolic succession, conferred approval on the entire independent movement of which he was the head, and brought the Polish National Catholic Church into the family of Old Catholic churches, which continues to this day. ("Old Catholic churches" are those that have retained certain distinctive doctrines and customs of the Roman Catholic Church, while rejecting the authority of the pope and repudiating those decisions of the Council of Trent and later councils which conflict with "ancient Catholic principles.") Soon after the formation of the Polish National Catholic Church, Bishop Hodur instituted the use of Polish in the Mass and established a theological seminary, named after the Italian reformer Savonarola. In 1921 a General Synod abolished mandatory clerical celibacy. Hodur, as Prime Bishop, remained their leader until his death in 1953.

The PNCC continues to nurture its people in their Polish cultural heritage. For example, the PNCC General Synod encourages support for a Music Scholarship Fund, which was established by the United Choirs Organization, and has an active Commission on History and Archives. Since 1908 an insurance organization, the Polish National Union, has worked hand-in-hand with the PNCC, and they jointly operate Spojnia Manor, a resident care facility in Waymart, Pennsylvania.

Major Doctrines

The PNCC declared at its second General Synod in 1906 the hearing of the Word of God as preached by the church to be a sacrament along with the traditional sacraments. Confirmation is considered an affirmation of Baptism. PNCC doctrine is based upon the Bible, the first four Ecumenical Councils, teachings of the early Church Fathers, and the Niceno-Constantinople Creed and its further interpretations by the Synod of the church. It is expounded in the "Profession of Faith," to which church members must assent. The church rejects the doctrine of the infallibility of the pope in matters of faith and morals; it encourages the individual to read Scripture.

Followers of the Supreme Being are "capable of attaining a certain degree of the happiness and of the perfection which is possessed of God in an infinite degree"; faith is helpful toward salvation, though not absolutely necessary, especially "blind faith"; good deeds bring people closer to God and Christ the Mediator and make them worthy of being followers and children of God. The doctrine of eternal punishment is rejected. As followers become closer to God, "sin will gradually grow less and less until it vanishes entirely" and the Kingdom of God will prevail upon earth.

Geography

At the time of secession the PNCC had less than 20,000 members, largely in the East. Organized in 1897, the PNCC's first Synod was held in 1904. The church grew rapidly in its early days, growing to over 61,000 members between 1916 and 1926. *The Yearbook of American and Canadian Churches* published a 1960 PNCC report of 162 parishes and 282,411 inclusive membership. The World Council of Churches handbook published in 1982 lists 100,000 members, 153 congregations and 5 dioceses. After World War I, the PNCC established a mission in Poland and built a theological seminary in Cracow. The church in Poland (the Polish Catholic Church) declared itself to be autocephalous in 1951, but has remained in communion with the American church. Czech and Slovak, Croatian, Lithuanian, Italian and Hungarian National Catholics were also organized. Though only a few parishes, all of the first four ethnic groups survived within the movement. Like other American churches with a strong ethnic origin, the Polish National Catholics in the United States and Canada were gradually faced with the question of openness to persons of other backgrounds, especially among youth today.

Organization

The church recognizes three orders in the ministry: bishops, priests and deacons. Administrative power is centralized in the bishops and Grand Council (clerical and lay). Highest authority is vested in the Synod, which meets in regular session every four years. Diocesan bishops of the five dioceses are elected by clergy and lay members of the Synod, while pastors of parishes are appointed by the bishop of the diocese. Each congregation is governed by an elected parish committee. Part of the heritage of Bishop Hodur is the synthesis of Catholic principles with a democratic ecclesiastical administration. Although the PNCC does not ordain women clergy, it upholds the rights of women in the administrative affairs of the church.

Worship

The PNCC has always been essentially Catholic in liturgy and worship. Worship in the Polish language was a key concern in the founding of the PNCC. As immigrant families entered second and third generations, however, the desire for an English liturgy increased, so that as early as 1937 English translations began to appear beside the Polish liturgy, and in July 1958 the Tenth General Synod decreed that parishes may institute the practice of having a Mass in English in addition to the Polish. In 1961 the English Mass was introduced and practiced throughout the church. Other liturgical changes and reforms followed that increased the participation of the people.

Ecumenical Involvement

The PNCC has always maintained friendly relations with other Christian churches in the U.S. and Europe. It established intercommunion with the Episcopal Church in 1946 and has had especially warm relations until the Episcopal Church's decision to ordain women caused the PNCC to terminate communion with it and the Anglican Church of Canada. Through mutual participation in the Union of Utrecht with the Old Catholic Churches, a dialogue of PNCC, Anglicans, and the Episcopal Church continues in a North American Working Group. The PNCC joined the National Council of Churches of Christ in the U.S.A. in 1957 and is a member also of the World Council of Churches. A PNCC representative has occasionally been an observer at the Consultation on Church Union. Dialogues with the Roman Catholic Church are undertaken with the National Conference of Catholic Bishops. The recent meetings in Columbia, South Carolina, with the pope were warmly reported by representatives from the PNCC.

The Prime Bishop John F. Swantek, in a forthright statement January 30, 1988, printed in the PNCC news organ *God's Field*, reminded his people of the unity of Christ's body expressed in the PNCC Confession of Faith and in the "Eleven Great Principles of the Polish National Catholic Church":

We must never harbor ill will forever. I have experienced the unpleasantness of the past among Church people, and I want it to remain in the past, for I prefer to see different Christian people from all Churches interacting and working together in many areas. The world has too many problems as it is without the Church adding to them. Instead, the followers of our Lord can work together to resolve the problems which may be plaguing the people of this day and age.

Noting a "mutual respect now surfacing among followers of Christ from separated churches," he urged the PNCC, with the aid of the Holy Spirit, to be willing to be used to actualize Christian unity.

THE PRESBYTERIAN CHURCH (U.S.A.)

In 1988 Presbyterians celebrated the 200th anniversary of the organization of a General Assembly in the newly-declared United States of America and the newly-named "Presbyterian Church in the United States of America." Yet Presbyterian Puritans were among the earliest settlers in Virginia, Maryland, Pennsylvania, New Jersey and New England about 150 years before that formal organization. They were influential and instrumental in the American Revolution — so much so that a prominent Presbyterian minister, John Witherspoon, was a signer of the Declaration of Independence.

They had come from England, Scotland, Ireland, and parts of Europe, where the Reformed views of the Frenchman John Calvin had flourished. Just as the protest of Luther touched off the tinder of discontent in Germany, so the reforming Protestant movement reached Calvin in France. He fled to Switzerland away from Catholic persecution and wrote, at the age of twenty-seven, his remarkable *Institutes of the Christian Religion.* Persuaded by a Protestant minister, Farel, to stay and labor in Geneva, Calvin spent much of his career there, where he experimented with democratic concepts and designs for civic and church government and thus developed one of Presbyterianism's most distinctive attributes. Followers of Calvinism, whether Huguenots in France, Hungarian Reformers, "beggars" of the Reformed Church in the Netherlands, Waldensians in

Italy, Covenanters and Seceders and Presbyterians in Scotland and Ireland, Puritan Presbyterians in England, or Calvinistic Methodists in Wales, were subject to outward persecution and inward division. Many sought new religious space in the colonies of North America, a desire that broadened gradually into a concern for religious liberty.

Already separated by different geographic origins, Presbyterian settlers in America became more deeply divided during the First Great Awakening of pre-Revolutionary times into "Old Side" and "New Side" (revivalistic) Presbyterians. Although reunited in 1758, they suffered another division between "Old School" and "New School" from 1837 to 1869, years of national geographic expansion, that hampered their ability to respond to national opportunity despite strong missionary spirit. Determination to send into the frontier an educated ministry also restricted the rapidity of growth of Presbyterianism, but that nevertheless enhanced its educational influence. Soon after Confederate forces bombarded Fort Sumter in 1861, the "Old School" divided once again for complex reasons that included slavery and support of the Federal cause. New School Presbyterians had already divided over slavery, but by 1864 the Old School and New School churches had reunited in the South to form the Presbyterian Church in the United States.

After the war northern Presbyterians of both "schools" reunited in 1869, drawn together by the necessities of war, the challenges of mission, and theological shifts. Meanwhile the independent, strong-spirited Covenanters and Seceders of Scotland, who had settled in America and formed their own churches, such as the Associate Reformed Church, had gathered in 1858 to become the United Presbyterian Church of North America. Some continue even to this day as the Associate Reformed Church. A hundred years later this vigorous United Presbyterian Church of North America merged (1958) with the Presbyterian Church in the U.S.A. to form the United Presbyterian Church in the U.S.A. They brought with them three seminaries, six U.S. colleges, and a breadth of mission churches in Asia and Africa. In turn, the Presbyterian Church in the U.S.A., having previously merged with some Cumberland Presbyterians, was already noted for its theological and social action vigor, mission endeavors and educational institutions. Extended negotiations of the United Presbyterian Church in the U.S.A. and the southern Presbyterian Church of the U.S. culminated in 1983, after 122 years of separation, in joyous reunion in Atlanta. Some complex details of unity were left to work out in the future, one of which has been the decision in 1987 to relocate the united headquarters in Louisville, Kentucky. A few churches sought refuge from unity by joining the Presbyterian Church in America (org. 1973), but the vast majority of Presbyterians were at last in one denominational fold.

Major Doctrines

Like other Reformers, Presbyterians emphasize dependence upon God as Creator, Redeemer, Judge and Sanctifier. Calvin's *Institutes*, structured around the Apostles' Creed, stress God's sovereignty over all of life, including human structures and powers. Thus Presbyterians join the Holy Spirit, God's active agent bearing witness to Jesus Christ, in bringing about a transformation in all areas of human consciousness and human endeavor. Christians are called to obedience not to become saved, but because they are saved. The Westminster Confession, once the chief summary of doctrine and faith along with the Larger and Shorter Catechism, now joins a "Book of Confessions," which includes the "Confession of 1967" as well as the Apostles' and Nicene Creeds, Scottish and Heidelberg Confessions, and the Barmen Declaration. "A Declaration of Faith" was commended for study and use in the Presbyterian Church U.S. in 1976 and is widely used today.

Geography

Some 3.1 million Presbyterians worship across the nation in about 11,600 churches, only 19 percent of which have more than 400 members, 45 percent have 100–400 members, and 36 percent fewer than 100. However, about half of the church's membership is still in congregations of 500 or more. There are still large concentrations of Presbyterians around Pittsburgh, Pennsylvania, and Charlotte, North Carolina. A recent research profile of churches reveals that a vast majority of Presbyterian congregations contain only a small percentage of racial or ethnic minority persons or none at all; those with the largest number tend to be located in the West and South Central regions (especially Hispanic and Asian) and the South.

Organization

The Presbyterian form of church government is a connectional system of courts: the local church session, the Presbytery (a lay/clerical body so distinctive as to provide the name for "Presbyterianism" and the heart of the connectional system), Synods (regional), and the General Assembly, which meets annually and is composed of clergy and laity named as delegates from the Presbyteries. There are no bishops, but elders and deacons are ordained through a laying on of hands by the session and are elected by the congregation. A moderator is elected annually to serve the General Assembly for the successive year. The stated clerk and ministry directors are also elected by the General Assembly. Women have been eligible for ordination into ministry since 1956 in the United Presbyterian Church of the U.S.A. and since 1964 in the Presbyterian Church in the U.S. (southern).

Worship

Consistent with the emphasis upon an educated clergy, worship among Presbyterians focuses strongly upon the reading and preaching of the Scripture, so that the exposition of the Word, the sermon, is the central event. Sacraments, especially the Lord's Supper, are revered as outward symbols with inward meaning, but only in recent years has there been more frequent celebration to nourish the faith, the Lord's Supper having been observed as little as semiannually in many Presbyterian churches. There is a *Directory for the Worship of God*, a constitutional document for the guidance of public worship, as well as *The Book of Common Worship;* these, in addition to the *Book of Order*, are normative documents for the church.

Ecumenical Involvement

The ecumenical spirit that kept a fracturing church reuniting toward increased wholeness was and is at work among Presbyterians in the larger church. Many individual Presbyterians were active in the voluntary societies of the nineteenth century, like the American Home Missionary Society, the American Board of Commissioners for Foreign Mission, the American Bible Society, the Evangelical Alliance and the American Sunday School Union, which were nondenominational. A unique Plan of Union existed between Presbyterians and Congregationalists for a number of years. Gradually a denominational spirit induced even the Presbyterians to develop their own missions effort. In 1958, when the United Presbyterian Church in the U.S.A. was formed, the Commission on Ecumenical Mission and Relations was established, which expressed a new concept of relations with sister churches and joint mission with them as a fresh approach to "foreign missions." They were also fully involved in founding the Federal Council of Churches and later the National and World Councils of Churches. It was Eugene Carson Blake, then Presbyterian stated clerk and later general secretary of the WCC, whose vision and public challenge brought the Consultation on Church Union into existence in 1962. Presbyterians contribute an educated clergy, a zeal for the Scriptures, a strong mission spirit, social concern, a will toward unity, a talent for orderliness, respect for God's sovereignty over all of life, and an involved laity as special gifts to the ecumenical church.

REFORMED CHURCH IN AMERICA

When the Dutch West India Company came to North America in 1624, it developed the colony of New Netherland on Manhattan Island along the Hudson River, named after the English explorer Henry Hudson, who was dispatched by Dutch merchants to find a route to the Indies. Soon after the first colonists, with their Kranken-Besoeckers ("visitors of the sick"), came Governor Peter Minuit's traders, followed by Jonas Michaelius, the first pastor, who, in 1628, organized a congregation of Dutch and Walloon communicants. He conducted services in both Dutch and French. In 1650, after clashes between Native Americans and some of the colonists in 1643, two-thirds of the European population was destroyed and there were only three Dutch Reformed congregations left — New Amsterdam, Fort Orange (Albany) and Newcastle. One prominent minister, Johannes Megapolensis, serving on the van Rennselaer landholdings, learned the Mohawk tongue and did missionary work among the Indians.

When the English took over the middle colonies in 1664, the Duke of York ("New York") allowed freedom of worship and did not interfere in Dutch church affairs. At the turn of the century (1700) there were twenty-nine Reformed congregations to only one newly-formed Anglican parish, Trinity, which was founded in what is now the financial district of lower Manhattan; by 1720 the Reformed churches had increased to fifty.

The storm center of Reformed Church life in the eighteenth century was the right to ordain. Until 1747 the Dutch church was supervised by the Classis (Presbytery) of Amsterdam. Deeply influenced by the Great Awakening, ardent reformist Theodorus Jacobus Frelinghuizen wanted to establish an American Coetus (classis) to speed the process of ordination. Ultra-Dutch dominies countered with a Conferentie; they wanted their ministers trained in the Netherlands, despite the arduous journey. Utrecht-trained John Henry Livingston led in working out a compromise that resolved this controversy of several decades. As a result, the first separate divinity school in the U.S. was founded in 1784, initially in New York and later in New Brunswick, New Jersey, and the right of ordination was transferred from the Classis of Amsterdam.

The Dutch church, like many others that were established with a cultural and ethnic identity, gradually adjusted to being an American church, although the Dutch language predominated into the first quarter of the nineteenth century. Once divided in attitudes toward the American Revolution, the Dutch church changed its name from Reformed Protestant Dutch Church to Reformed Dutch Church in 1819 and then in 1867 to the Reformed Church in America.

A second wave of Dutch immigrants came in the mid-1800s, this time fleeing religious persecution. Some entire congregations came with their "Dominie" (pastor). Hendrick Pieter Scholte, for example, brought his young bride and his congregation to an open prairie, which became Pella ("City of Refuge"), Iowa, still today a stronghold of the Reformed Church. Another was Albertus Christianus Van Raalte, who wrote to the Provincial Synod of Zuid-Holland in 1835, "The voice of my conscience and the infallible sayings of the holy Scriptures compelled me some time ago to break all ecclesiastical union with you, and to join those who by word and deed prove their desire to live according to God's ordinances, the opposite of which is taking place in the Reformed denomination." King William, trying to maintain a delicate balance between the Belgians, predominantly Roman Catholic, and the Dutch, predominantly Reformed, could not satisfy the conservatives who sought traditional doctrine and practice and a return to governmental relationships prior to the outcome of the wars of 1812. Recent scholarship by Gerrit J. tenZythoff suggests that unresolved issues of this period, which included a Dutch Awakening ("Reveil"), contributed to the division in America in 1857 that produced the Christian Reformed Church. Many second-wave settlers went to Michigan and Iowa. A third wave in the 1950s went largely to Canada and did much to strengthen the Christian Reformed Church as well as the Reformed Church there.

In recent years the Reformed Church has sought to become increasingly diverse ethnically and culturally, especially in urban areas, and has made a priority of "Crossing Cultural Barriers: Reaching and Receiving in Christ." The church has had a strong world mission effort. It is currently involved in approximately twenty-five countries, including India, Japan, the Middle East, Africa, Mexico, and with Chinese-speaking populations in various countries. The Reformed Church in America is attempting to redefine its mission interest to include receiving as well as sending missionaries. It has also become more concerned about the role of the church in such social issues as peace, world hunger, family life, and the changing roles of women and men in church and society. It views itself as both "ecumenical" and "evangelical" as it develops close linkage of its "On the Way" evangelism focus with its programs of Christian education and social witness. The Reformed Church in America is deeply concerned about the Reformed churches of South Africa, with whom it shares a common Dutch heritage, and is particularly concerned today for the Black Reformed churches.

Major Doctrines

The constitution of the Reformed Church in America consists of the Doctrinal Standards, the Liturgy, and Government. The Doctrinal Standards are the Heidelberg Catechism (written to bring Lutherans and Reformed in Germany together and adopted by the Dutch Reformed Church), the Belgic Confession (a moving personal statement of Calvinism by Guido de Bres in 1561), and the Canons of the Synod of Dort. The Apostles' and Nicene Creeds are also recognized; these creeds and the

Heidelberg Catechism are still important for parishioners today, according to a recent survey. The inspired word of God is the "only rule of faith and practice." Covenant theology, the primacy of God's grace, and the sovereignty of God are important Reformed emphases.

Geography

In 1987 there were 957 churches with an inclusive membership of 346,846 located in the United States and Canada. Early settlements in New York and New Jersey, the Midwest — especially Iowa and Michigan — and more recently in California and other western states are strong areas of the Reformed Church. Today there are not only Dutch, but Black, Hispanic, Asian, Indian, Native American, and other European backgrounds represented in the church. A recent study by Donald Luidens and Roger Nemeth identified 47 percent of respondents whose families were members of the RCA when they were sixteen years old, with those in Middle America most strongly so identified (60 percent).

Organization

The local church is governed by a consistory. Several consistories send representatives to a classis, like a Presbytery. Particular Synods are regional, and the General Synod meets annually. *The Book of Church Order* establishes these structures, functions, disciplines and responsibilities. Preparation for ministry requires supervision both by the classis and by professors of the seminary, and pastors must assent to the Doctrinal Standards as well as the Ecumenical Creeds. Ministers have university and seminary training (including Greek and Hebrew).

Worship

As in other Reformed churches, the preaching of the Word is the focal act of worship. Church members have typically obtained more education than Americans generally, and the clergy are expected to be well educated. Worship is dignified, but there is room for considerable variation of ordering the service. In the sacraments (Lord's Supper and Baptism), the presence of the Holy Spirit gives reality to the promises of God, and it is God's promise that in the celebration of the sacraments Christ, through the power of the Spirit, is indeed present.

Ecumenical Involvement

There have been repeated attempts to unite the Dutch Reformed with other Reformed churches. Cultural and linguistic differences foiled early efforts to unite German and Dutch churches. Efforts in 1920 to unite with the Presbyterian Church in the U.S.A. found little response, as the RCA held firmly to its distinctive Dutch confessional standards. After World War II, attempts were made to unite with the United Presbyterian Church, but the RCA lacked the necessary two-thirds majority of classes. A merger with the southern Presbyterian Church also failed by a margin of one vote in one classis! The Reformed Church in America is, however, staunchly ecumenical. It has been party to most ecumenical organizations since their inception, including the National and World Councils of Churches and the World Alliance of Reformed Churches. Although it is not a member of the Consultation of Church Union, it has been an observer and came very close in 1987 to voting favorably for membership. The RCA has recently given its general approbation to the "Baptism, Eucharist and Ministry" document.

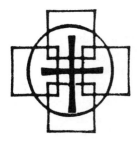

GENERAL CONVENTION
OF THE NEW JERUSALEM
(THE SWEDENBORGIAN CHURCH)

A tricentennial symposium on science and metaphysics, a Swedenborg film festival, and a pictorial anthology of the "World of Swedenborg" were among the events that marked the three hundredth birthday of Emanuel Swedenborg in 1988. Son of a Lutheran bishop in Stockholm, Sweden, born in 1688, Emanuel Swedenborg had keen interest in religion as a child but developed an early career in science. Assessor of Mines for the Royal Swedish government, he made scholarly scientific contributions in mathematics, chemistry, physics, astronomy and anatomy, as well as geology and mineralogy.

Highly respected as a pioneering scientist, Swedenborg was an aristocrat and long-time member of the Swedish Parliament. At the age of fifty-seven he underwent a personally troubling reorientation away from science (which he had studied with an "ulterior motive" of combatting by scientific and rationalistic methods the scientific and rationalistic materialism of his day, says chronicler Marguerite Block) toward spiritual experience and interpretation. He studied with scientific detachment his disturbing dreams, visions and visitations, making copious notes, and he learned the languages necessary for rigorous biblical study.

53

Swedenborg's study of dreams contributed toward the emerging discipline of psychology; his recorded experiences of spiritual contact with angels and departed religious figures caused some of his nineteenth-century followers, in the view of other Swedenborgians, to be overly receptive to Mesmer and other spiritualists. His distinctive view of Christianity brought harsh criticism from traditional churches, some people even charging that he had become demented. Yet his stature in society, in the field of science, and in intellectual circles made him difficult to dismiss, and a small but distinguished following persisted after his death.

Immanuel Tafel, a German scholar, founded a New Church in Germany, although Swedenborg did not intend to found a church but to reinvigorate Christianity and to integrate his insights into existing Christian churches as "The New Church." In England, where religious tolerance allowed his works to be published although banned in Sweden, Robert Hindmarsh and others intrigued with Swedenborgian thought formed reading circles or "Theosophical Societies," some remaining in the Anglican or Methodist churches and others separating from them. In 1787 the separatists acquired a Dissenter's License and the New Church (of the New Jerusalem) was established in England; England is considered the real birthplace and mother of other branches of the New Church.

In Philadelphia in 1784, soon after American independence, James Glen became a missionary of the New Church by publishing a newspaper ad for "a discourse on the extraordinary science of celestial and terrestrial connections and correspondences, recently revived by the late honorable and learned Emanuel Swedenborg." Among those who showed sufficient interest to subscribe to the publication of an English edition of Swedenborg's *True Christian Religion* was Benjamin Franklin. Hetty Barclay, sister-in-law of an early Pennsylvania follower of Swedenborg, has the distinction of being the first real New Churchwoman in the world, and one of the first subscriber's to Robert Hindmarsh's *Magazine of Knowledge*. Swedenborg's writing attracted followers in Philadelphia, Baltimore, New York and Boston, where small numbers of intellectuals formed New Church societies, and there were a few individuals in the South who responded to his ideas. Support for freeing of slaves was an important outcome of Swedenborg's thought among followers not only in the South but also in England and Europe; there was even an abortive effort to found a colony on the west coast of Africa.

Swedenborgianism travelled westward to the frontier of the United States through such unlikely messengers as Johnny Appleseed, who, as well as planting the seeds of apples, left chapters of Swedenborg's writings at pioneer cabins along his horseback journeys. The new doctrines were also spread by pastors of various traditions who found Swedenborg's work stimulating. But New England was the richest soil for planting his ideas. Emerson, who mourned the lack of poetry in Swedenborg, still found his concepts worthy of presentation, although he never became a Swedenborgian. Brook Farm Transcendentalists found Swedenborgian thinkers congenial, and some New Church followers were attracted to the utopian socialism of Robert Owen. Fourierism and Homeopathy were also new systems of thought that found Swedenborg's ideas to share some affinities. Troubling, however, was the effort to make Swedenborg a "father of spiritualists," who believed in animal magnetism or hypnosis, in trances and séances for engaging in dialogue with the dead. Swedenborg, though agreeing with Mesmerism and spiritualism about the reality of the spiritual world and the spirituality of human beings, warned against seeking out intercourse with spirits. He never sought to converse with angels and spirits, but found himself a recipient of their initiative.

Ecclesiastically, a national body began to take form in the United States in 1817, when the first General Convention of the New Jerusalem in the U.S.A. gathered in Philadelphia, bringing together seventeen societies with approximately 360 members. By 1890 there were 154 societies and 7,095 members. Like other human organizations, the New Church experienced some dissention, especially over the issue of pastoral relationships with a congregation, which Boston pastor Thomas Worcester interpreted as equivalent to marriage — the "conjugial heresy." The issue of centralized power was especially sensitive to persons attracted to the freedom of individual thought that was epitomized in Swedenborg's own inquiry. In mid-nineteenth century, the General Convention had two competing conventions — Western and Central, but eventually divisive issues (e.g., regulation of the clergy and rules of the convention — which became only recommendations) were resolved. A schism did, however, occur over the authority of Swedenborg, and the General Church of the New Jerusalem was formed in 1897 to assert that Swedenborg was not only divinely illumined but also divinely inspired, and that his writings have the status of divine authority.

The General Convention began a school, Urbana University, a pioneer in co-education, in Urbana, Ohio, in 1850. There are also Swedenborg book centers in Philadelphia and Boston, and a Foundation in New York City, which respond to inquiries from around the world for Swedenborg's writings. In recent years the New Church has undergone restructure and reassessment of its mission, which, through the vision and instrumentality of Swedenborg, works on many issues of social concern as part of the new heaven and the new earth that are the continual Second Coming.

Swedenborg's thought, his "heavenly doctrines," are found in such major writings as *Arcana Coelestia, True Christian Religion, Heaven and Hell* and others, thirty volumes in the standard English edition. Notables such as Helen Keller have found their faith there, and intellectuals and literary figures such as William Blake, Henry James, Edgar Allen Poe, the Brownings, Balzac, and Samuel Taylor Coleridge have been influenced by him. The late Jorge Luis Borges, blind Argentinian writer of world stature, wrote of Swedenborg in a poem, "He would see that which earthly eyes do not see: the fierce geometry, the crystal labyrinth of God and the sordid milling of infernal delights...."

Major Doctrines

Robert H. Kirven, past president of the Swedenborg School of Religion, says:

The theological position of the General Convention is distinguished by the contributions of Emanuel Swedenborg,

18th-century scientist, mystic, and biblical theologian. The thrust of his contemporary reforms — correcting trinitarian thinking to restore a proper emphasis on the oneness of God, elevating the status of the Bible as the Word of the Lord, and emphasizing the inter-dependent unity of faith and works — continue to characterize the Convention's theology.

Swedenborg's central emphasis on the inner levels of meaning of the Scriptures, by which a fuller understanding of God is available, does not disparage the outer scriptural meaning. He attempted not to set forth new religious doctrine but to expand the insights of the Bible. For example, Swedenborg understood the Second Coming not as an actual physical reappearance, but Christ's return in spirit and truth that is being effected as a present reality, thus still taking place. His understanding of heaven and hell have been particularly attractive interpretations for explorers of his thought. Death, he says, is an entry into consciousness of the spiritual world to which we have been largely unconscious in the material world. His understanding of the mystery of the Divine Trinity asserts that "these three, Father, Son, and Holy Spirit, are the three essentials of one God, and they make one as soul, body, and operation make one in man [humanity]."

Geography

Stretching from Canada to Guyana, the General Convention membership in North America at the end of 1986 was forty-seven societies with fifty ordained clergy and a membership of 2,295 — 1,799 of whom are active. There are independent bodies in close communication with the General Convention in continental Europe (the Continental Association of the New Church), the Philippines, Japan, Korea, Mexico, several Latin American countries, East and West Indies, India, and Burma, with the largest national membership to be found in Black South Africa. There are also several thousand members in the British Isles. In the U.S., the states of Massachusetts and Illinois and the Pacific Coast have the largest number of societies.

American Swedenborgians have experimented in new forms of church programming for a dispersed and relatively small number of adherents. For example, the Wayfarers' Chapel along the Pacific coast, a stunning glass and redwood chapel, attracts visitors from around the world and is the setting for many weddings. "Bostonview," built upon the site of the first Boston Church of the New Jerusalem on Beacon Hill, is a multi-story apartment house that helps sustain the church sanctuary and library on the first floors.

Organization

Operating under a congregational form of government, individual churches or "societies" belong to regional associations. Each year delegates from each church are chosen to participate in the annual meeting of the regional association, which sends participants to the annual national convention. National convention delegates vote concerning resolutions, constitutional amendments and election of national officers and committee members. Both ministers and lay are eligible for all offices, but there is also an inclusive Council of Ministers to handle matters of worship, doctrine and ministry. In 1975 the first woman was ordained to ministry. The recent restructure streamlines administration, supports local initiatives, and attempts to undergird the spiritual well-being of people, including their human rights as well as physical and material well-being.

Worship

Baptism and the Holy Supper are recognized by Swedenborgians as "two gates to eternal life," but without "magical" significance. Baptism in other churches is recognized and Communion is open, although rebaptism and closed Communion were an early practice of some societies. In England the first liturgies were modeled on the Church of England and published in 1788, the third edition being the model for the first American New Church liturgy published in Baltimore in 1792. Swedenborgian theology is incorporated in the liturgies. Since then there have been numerous liturgies and worship books published for the New Jerusalem Church, the Boston Society 1829 version having scriptural chants but no hymns. Some worship books contained more ritual forms than others. The 1982 looseleaf edition includes two sacraments and three rites — Confirmation, Marriage and Resurrection — while the 1950 book added Burial, Ordination, Installation and Investiture.

Ecumenical Involvement

The Swedenborgian Church is a member of the National Council of Churches. It recognizes all Christian ordinations. The New Church manifests an ecumenical breadth of spirit and its Swedenborgian theology emphasizes the responsibility of each person to develop his or her own beliefs and to live life accordingly, while respecting the similar rights and responsibilities of others.

2

AMERICAN ORIGIN CHURCHES

AMERICAN BAPTIST CHURCHES IN THE U.S.A.

Although Baptists look to no single leader or event that constitutes their origins, some trace Baptists back to Bible times, others to the "radical" ideas of such Anabaptist leaders as Manz, Sattler, and Hubmaier (put to death, as were the wives of the latter two, for concepts of voluntary religion and believer's Baptism in the sixteenth century), and some to the English Puritan Separatists and Congregationalists.

One such Separatist leader, John Smyth, fled England for Holland with a little band of followers in 1607. Two years later he accepted the Baptism of believers and baptized himself and about forty others, thus founding the first English Baptist congregation, part of whom were led back to England in 1611 by Thomas Helwys and became the source of the tradition called General Baptists because of its belief that Christ died for all. Another group of Baptists, organized in London by John Spilsbury, a Congregationalist, was called Particular Baptists because of their Calvinist belief in predestination, as they asserted that Christ died only for the elect. Both groups, under severe persecution until the Toleration Act of 1689, eventually merged to form the Baptist Union of Great Britain in 1891.

The first U.S. Baptist congregation was organized in 1638 in Providence, Rhode Island, through the assistance of Roger Williams. Both General (Arminian) and Particular (Calvinist)

Baptists flourished in the U.S. In 1707 the Philadelphia Baptist Association was formed and became the first Baptist association, which under Quaker religious toleration grew rapidly and became a model for Baptist organization. Baptists from the North moved to South Carolina and continued their witness. Other Baptists from England were establishing churches in Virginia. In the early nineteenth century various Black Baptist associations were formed, paving the way for the rapid growth of independent denominations after the Civil War. However, there are many Blacks who play their role in the Black church today through participation in the ABC.

Special attention has been paid in the late 1980s to three key anniversaries crucial to the development of the American Baptist churches: 1987 — the 175th anniversary of the sailing of pioneer missionaries Ann and Adoniram Judson and Luther Rice; 1988 — the 200th birthday of Adoniram Judson; and 1989 — the 175th anniversary of the formation of the General Missionary Convention of the Baptist Denomination in the U.S. for Foreign Missions. Ann Judson boldly slipped beside her new husband to kneel for the ordination prayer before their sea voyage to India as Congregational missionaries. Before the end of their voyage, Adoniram had become converted to Baptist views, and Ann, soon after landing, agreed. Luther Rice, after consultation with Judson and William Carey, noted English Baptist missionary, soon changed his views, too. In 1814 the General Missionary Convention was formed in the U.S. to support the Judsons in Burma — the first Baptist missionaries from American shores. Such missionary organizations, along with an American Baptist Home Mission Society and the American Baptist Publication Society, began to shape a denominational consciousness. Historian Warren Mild fairly states that "missions made American Baptists into a denomination."

This denominational consciousness was severely tested over the issue of slavery in 1845, however, when southerners withdrew to form the Southern Baptist Convention, whose greatest growth has occurred in the twentieth century. In the North, Baptists organized in 1907 the Northern Baptist Convention, later changed to the American Baptist Convention (1950) and once again renamed the American Baptist Churches in the U.S.A. in 1972. Growing out of the national missionary and educational agencies, the Northern Convention gave the member churches a base for joining the Federal Council of Churches. It also sought "to give expression to the opinions of its constituency upon moral, religious and denominational matters and to promote denominational unity and efficiency in efforts for the evangelization of the world."

Baptists in England and the United States have had a noble ministry to the disinherited of society, challenging the social order to become just and to put inequalities under the reforming light of the Gospel. William Knibb fought against slavery in Jamaica, while Robert Hall, Joseph Ivimey and Francis Cox worked to improve factory "sweat shop" conditions in England. John Howard (prison reform) was followed in the United States by John Mason Peck (churches, schools and roads in the Midwest), Isaac McCoy (American Indian missions), and — best known of all — Walter Rauschenbusch, who brought Christian conscience and compassion into the vast social marketplace.

Major Doctrines

Like other Baptist groups the ABC bases membership upon mutual covenant rather than on official creed, although some congregations and associations use some sort of creedal statement. The belief in the competence of the soul, in the right and freedom of individual conscience, derived from the priesthood of all believers and reading of Scripture under the guidance of the Holy Spirit, is fundamental to Baptist understanding. Creeds are considered to be only human, thus inadequate, and give an intellectual formulation to a living faith. Baptists hold that church membership is composed of regenerate people who confess the experience of rebirth and are baptized on profession of personal faith in Jesus Christ as Lord and Savior. Religious liberty is another major Baptist conviction, as is the autonomy of the local church. They also acknowledge the freedom and sovereignty of God. Baptist groups emphasize and nuance the concepts of soul competency, human freedom, religious liberty, local church autonomy, and God's liberty in different ways, ac-

counting for some of the great variety of Baptist associations
and independent churches in the world. There are also varied
understandings of Holy Scripture, but it is always central to the
faith.

Geography

The network of Baptist churches around the world testifies
to the vigor of Baptist missionary spirit. In the Baptist World
Alliance there are over 33,000,000 Baptists in Europe, Africa,
the Middle East, Asia, Oceania, and the Americas. (There are
also at least 6,000,000 Baptists outside the Alliance.) North
American Baptists number over 27 million. The American
Baptist Churches in the U.S.A. in 1987 had a membership of
1,601,022 and 5,781 churches, remaining quite stable even as
various groups joined or departed its relatively loose convention over the years. It is possible to be a member of the ABC
and also of another Baptist convention or of a non-Baptist denomination. As befits a church first organized as the Northern
Baptist Convention, it is stronger in the northern part of the
U.S., although there are some churches in the South.

Organization

The ABC stands firmly in the free church tradition, although
it balances the independence of the local congregation with
its interdependence with other churches to avoid isolated self-
sufficiency and to acknowledge participation in the church universal. Such relationships require a very delicate equilibrium
with occasional adjustments, especially as the ABC has moved
in recent years to establish a more centralized organization, national program agencies, and a representative polity (1972 organizational restructure). The legislative body is the General
Board, a representative group of 208 members with one member elected by each of 151 election districts and the remainder
elected by the Board itself. The national program agencies or
boards, which at one time were independent national mission
societies, function as corporate entities under the authority of
the General Board. The General Staff Council serves as imple-
menting body for policies of the General Board. The general sec-

retary is the chief administrative officer. There are thirty-seven regional organizations (mostly state and city bodies) affiliated with the ABC, which also carry out a major part of the denominational program, covenanting to work in relationship with one another and with the national boards in most instances.

Worship

In the free church tradition Spirit is emphasized over form and ceremony, and evangelical expression of the Gospel is dominant over the sacramental. Baptists have no sacraments. The two ordinances observed by Baptists are Baptism and the Lord's Supper. Although dubbed "Baptists" by others, the Baptist tradition focuses upon the voluntary receiving of Christ as Lord and Savior, thus emphasis is placed upon believer's Baptism. Baptism of believers is a meaningful, initiatory rite in relation to church membership, an acted parable of new life, and is not a ceremony for infants. Immersion in water is the only scriptural mode of Baptism and symbolizes resurrection into new life with Christ. The Lord's Supper is an acted parable of spiritual nurture and is observed in memory of the sufferings of Christ. American Baptists practice open Communion, because they believe Jesus invites all to the table. Some ABC churches recognize the baptismal rites of other denominations, even if not by immersion, but Baptism by immersion is regarded as biblical and normative as well as beautiful and meaningful. Some others do not require Baptism as a condition of church membership.

Ecumenical Involvement

American Baptists are prominent among all Baptists for their strong ecumenical commitment, which stems from their understanding of the basic nature of their church as "a manifestation of the church universal," according to an enlarged Statement of Purpose adopted in 1969. They are members of the Baptist World Alliance, the North American Baptist Fellowship, and the Baptist Joint Committee on Public Affairs. They are founding members of the National and World Councils of Churches, as well as predecessor interdenominational agencies. The ABC has not voted to join the Consultation on Church Union, but it does participate in the American Bible Society, Religion in American Life, and the Joint Strategy and Action Committee. In 1975 the General Board commended for study "A Rationale for Appropriate Support of Ecumenical Bodies," along with a statement by its Committee on Christian Unity of the General Board on "An Understanding of Christian Unity," with guidelines for interchurch relations. The statement expresses an ecumenical commitment to be responsible to and for one another, to perceive ecumenism as a response to Christ's Gospel, and to be open to the voice and Spirit of God through one another.

THE CHRISTIAN CHURCH
(DISCIPLES OF CHRIST)

In Kansas City, Missouri, on September 28, 1968, the Christian Churches (Disciples of Christ) became the Christian Church (Disciples of Christ), acknowledging with only two alphabetical letters a historic transition both theologically and philosophically to its becoming a church, a denomination, rather than a reforming ecumenical movement.

An outgrowth of the English-speaking Protestant Reformation in an era of feisty American freedom and insights of the Enlightenment, the movement was envisioned in the minds of three Presbyterian ministers: Barton Warren Stone, and Thomas and Alexander Campbell (father and son). Stone's experience of spiritual renewal at a Cane Ridge, Kentucky, gathering of 20,000 people, the largest of the Second Great Awakening events, convinced him that the unity of the church is essential for effective mission and evangelism. He wrote *The Last Will and Testament of the Springfield Presbytery* in 1804 to liberate the church from ecclesiastical bondage for the sake of unity, and it has become a classic charter document of the Christian Church, a name he and his colleagues adopted to signal inclusiveness. (From these same roots grew one branch of the United Church of Christ.)

Meanwhile, Thomas Campbell, born in Ireland, came to the "new world" to live out his vision of unity only to discover even greater rancorous divisions in the church than those he had left

behind. Suspended for serving Communion too broadly among
Presbyterians of differing views, he formed "The Christian Association of Washington" (Pennsylvania) and in 1809 wrote the
Declaration and Address to set forth its goals for Christian unity.
His son Alexander, educated at Glasgow, preferred the name
"Disciples of Christ" and rapidly became the primary leader
in a Restoration movement seeking to lead the church toward
unity and to restore its biblical grounding in Scripture. By 1832
the followers of Stone and the Campbells found one another in
a joyous service of union in Lexington, Kentucky, leaving their
name and other unresolved matters blessedly ambiguous. Similar Disciples groups were taking shape in England, Scotland,
Ireland, Canada, New Zealand, Australia, Latin America, India,
Asia and Africa.

The movement grew rapidly in individualistic frontier rural and small town America, less well in the cities. Its flexibil-
ity and minimal structure served throughout the divisive years
of the Civil War to preserve the Disciples' unity even as they
disagreed over slavery. Paul Crow, Disciples ecumenist, says,
"Their message of freedom, diversity, individualism, humani-
tarian concern, a reasonable faith, simplicity in faith and worship was attractive to the pioneers and their heirs," so that by
1900 there were 1,120,000 members.

The vision of Christian unity and of the restoration of scriptural essentials was a double vision, however, capable of causing disagreement over which was primary, especially as discord
arose over the "essentials" of Scripture. Some Restorationists
became legalists, canonizing Alexander Campbell's *The Christian System* as a test of fellowship, which would have appalled
him. Over the years a group now called the Churches of Christ
began to pull away (1906); then Independent Christians began
their own schools and agencies (1935–1955), and, as the denomination took form through the *Provisional Design for the
Christian Church (Disciples of Christ)*, about a fourth of the
churches withdrew their names from the *Yearbook* between 1967
and 1968, an act seen by many Disciples as the tragic result of
a misinformed organized campaign.

The years 1960–1985 have been crucial for Disciples in the

formation and identity of the ecumenical dream that had not intended to become another denomination. Up to that time the churches had founded about 300 educational institutions, at least a tenth of which have survived, the largest being Texas Christian University. They had organized missionary societies, the one led by Caroline Neville Pearre (Christian Woman's Missionary Society) stimulating the formation of others. True to their sense of mutuality in the faith, they have understood the spiritual necessity of reciprocity also in world missions. Although bruised by the discord within their own ranks, they actively participated in nearly all new ecumenical ventures, like the Federal Council of Churches (1908), and were the first American church to form (1910) their own special agency for the promotion of Christian Unity, which became the Council on Christian Unity.

After the Civil War a sizeable number of Blacks became Disciples and organized their own fellowship through the leadership of Preston Taylor, who also founded the National Christian Missionary Convention, which united with the Christian Church (Disciples of Christ) structure in 1969. A National Convocation continues as a forum for Black concerns. Hispanic and Asian participation is also growing.

Major Doctrines

Founded upon the conviction that the church is essentially one, the movement was wary of creeds as divisive. "Where the Scriptures speak, we speak; where the Scriptures are silent; we are silent," was an early slogan. But the issues of inerrancy of Scripture, the use of musical instruments in church, and of the interpretation of what restoration of the primitive early church would require caused some congregations to turn aside from the vision of the unity of the church. For the majority who remained, however, doctrinal freedom, historical or critical study of Scripture, the church as the community responding to God's covenant and the centrality of Baptism and the Lord's Supper are important marks of the Disciples. The preamble of the *Design*, which is no longer considered "provisional," expresses for many an eloquent and adequate affirmation of faith, but it is not a requirement for membership. The yearning for unity, sobered by experience, is still central and vital.

Geography

In 1900 over 80 percent of the U.S. membership was located in nine midwestern and southwestern states, and even today some 60 percent is in eight midwest/southwest states, Texas having the most and Missouri second. There are Disciples congregations in seven Canadian provinces as well as forty-six states of the U.S., with a total membership of 1,106,692 in 1986 and 4,221 congregations. Membership includes 50,000 Blacks and roughly 500 predominantly Black congregations, 3,000 Hispanics with 30 congregations, about 1,000 American Asians, and a few Native Americans. Their ministries, always ecumenical and promoting partnership, development, and self-help, have been carried into over seventy countries around the world.

Organization

Historically each congregation has had its own governance, although each has lived and witnessed to regional and international concerns. An annual convention of churches provided guidance to general (i.e., national) work, and in 1920 competing missionary societies were united. The 1968 restructure process was an attempt to shape a biblically-informed organization that was both functional and developmental. Its local churches, regions, and general "manifestations" are equal expressions of the church; the dominion of the church belongs to Christ. Congregations have full property and program rights, but they also recognize mutual covenantal interdependence and responsibility. There is a biennial General Assembly to which all Disciples have access, but only representatives vote. A 180-member General Board meets annually and a 44-member Administrative Committee meets twice a year. The top staff officer is general minister and president, and a moderator is elected for two years.

Worship

Because of a strong tradition of congregationalism, each congregation is free to worship as it chooses. There is, however, a common form of worship, which includes the proclamation of the Gospel, prayers of the people, hymns and anthems, and the celebration of the Lord's Supper. Kenneth Teegarden summarizes:

> We baptize by immersion, so we look like Baptists. We have Communion every Sunday, so we look a bit like Roman Catholics. We stress the ministry of the laity, so we look a little like Quakers. Our congregations call their pastors rather than accepting assigned ministers, so in that respect we look like Presbyterians. We rely heavily on preaching and teaching, so we look somewhat like Methodists. We have congregational government, so we look a lot like the United Church of Christ.

Believer's Baptism by immersion for the remission of sins is the general rule, but Disciples will recognize the Baptism of other churches. The Lord's Table, celebrated each Sunday and believed to be the central event in the life of the church, is open to all Christians; "Communion" or "Lord's Supper" are common terms, while "Eucharist" is only recently used. Remembrance (*anamnesis*), Christ's presence, the sign of Christ's mighty acts are all bound up in the spiritual reality of Communion, which is not tightly defined in doctrine.

Ecumenical Involvement
The Christian Church (Disciples of Christ) is a stimulus to ecumenism and has been an active participant in the National and World Councils, in the Consultation on Church Union, Joint Strategy and Action Committee, cooperative educational curricula and other innovative ecumenical efforts. They have developed an ecumenical partnership with the United Church of Christ and are engaged in international bilateral dialogues with the Roman Catholics (1977), the World Alliance of Reformed Churches, and the Russian Orthodox Church (1987). Through the years they have become increasingly involved in social issue concerns. At the world level Disciples churches from twenty-four countries relate to each other for ecumenical

witness through the Disciples Ecumenical Consultative Council. Perhaps the best recounting of the major contribution of the Disciples in ecumenism and the churches' involvement in social concerns is to recall significant Disciples who have been active contributors to ecumenical witness: Peter Ainslie, J. Irwin Miller, Roy G. Ross, Jean Woolfolk, Rosa Page Welch, George G. Beasley, Jr., Kenneth Teegarden, Albert Pennybacker, Paul A. L. Crow, Jr. — to name a few!

INTERNATIONAL COUNCIL
OF COMMUNITY CHURCHES

While there were Community Churches in the U.S. in the early 1800s, the movement was afforded significance in the early 1900s, when their numbers were in excess of one thousand. These churches grew in response to a variety of factors: over-churching, particularly in rural America, with its attendant economic and staff problems; also, restrictive denominational machinery that fed the desire for self-determination, laity activism, women's concerns, and the hunger for a relevant and unifying religion.

The first national organization in the movement was the Community Church Workers of the United States of America. Dating from mid-1923, chartered as "a service agency," headquartered first in surburban and then in downtown Chicago, it continued until mid-1936. Among its accomplishments were the establishing of the *Community Church Press* (reestablished in 1984) and the newspaper, *The Christian Community* (reestablished in 1948).

Chicago was the place and 1923 the time for commencing a second national organization, comprised of predominantly Black Community Churches incorporated as The Biennial Council of the People's Church of Christ and Community Centers of the United States of America and Elsewhere. In mid-1946, in Columbus, Ohio, the National Council of Community

Churches, predominantly White, was founded. In 1950, at a jointly held conference in Lake Forest and Chicago, these organizations merged to form the current International Council of Community Churches. It was a globally noteworthy racial integration of national religious bodies.

Major Doctrines

The Council seeks to protect and promote the right and responsibility of individual conscience. As Orvis F. Jordan, pastor and first president of the Community Church Workers of the U.S.A. said,

Community Churches need not believe a multitude of things. But what they do believe should be with a multitude of conviction. We must fix our faith in God. The Christ as the Savior of Souls and the Savior of Society must be our Master. The Bible as the textbook of our religion must be reverently studied. We shall seek to destroy no person's faith in the various doctrines which are consistent with these beginnings of faith, for the Community Church Movement is not an enemy to faith, though at times it might fight hurtful superstitions. In our churches, toleration of religious opinion is not inconsistent with deep-going loyalty.

The first president of the International Council of Community Churches, J. Ruskin Howe, adds:

A Community Church believes our statements of faith will be as personal and as varied as our individual experiences of God. Therefore, no one among us would assume to suggest that his or her statement of faith, or that of his or her church, must become a norm for other believers or other churches. As the Spirit itself is free and creative in each of our hearts, so our expression and description of that Spirit's work can neither be inherited from the past nor dictated by any ecclesiastical authority in the present. We believe in the living Christ at work in the heart of the individual believer. A Community Church recognizes in the historic creeds progressive efforts to put into words the meaning of eternal truth revealed in Jesus Christ. It does not, however, ascribe finality or infallibility to any human dogma. It affirms the right of each generation, each individual, and each church to restate in fresh contemporary terms the essence of its Christian faith.

The Council does not vote a church or center into or out of Council membership; a congregation makes this decision, based on its acceptance of the constitution and its willingness to enter into covenant with the Council and its congregational affiliates. The Council seeks to protect and promote the right and responsibility of individual congregational self-determination and self-government. There is no creedal statement with which a congregation must agree. Final authority in faith and order resides in persons as they relate to each other in local congregations.

Geography
There were 160 charter number congregations when, in 1950, the current Council began. While in the early part of the next three decades there was a membership increase, the period concluded with 77 members. Since 1980 there has been a 250 percent increase (350 member churches) over that lowest figure. Further, 25 percent of the member congregations have come into existence during this time. U.S.A. constituent membership is estimated at 200,000 of a total of 250,000. The Council provides services to churches and centers whether or not they are in Council membership. If these 1000 or so are taken into account, the U.S.A. constituent membership swells to an estimated 500,000. Some confusion is caused by the fact that 25 percent of the Council's members do not have "Community" in their names and that many who do use it are either denominational churches only or are independent of all national organizations.

Racial balance continues among the Council's members: In 1987 U.S.A. units were 54 percent predominantly White, 38 percent predominantly Black, 8 significantly integrated. There are a few Asian Americans. One-third of the Council's affiliates are outside the U.S., notably in Africa, and there are working relationships with Community Churches in other nations, such as the People's Republic of China. Furthermore, in 1987, 5 percent of the Council's members have resulted from federated or union churches, 5 percent are affiliated both with the Council and one or more denominations, 10 percent have resulted from withdrawal of congregations from denominations, and 80 percent have never had denominational alignments.

As these figures indicate, some Council members identify themselves as interdenominational or as multidenominational and others as nondenominational. Increasingly, "postdenominational" is the term utilized to signify a positive thankfulness for the good accomplished in and through denominations and a commitment to movement beyond divisiveness and competitiveness. A recent phenomenon is that some churches are composed mainly of former Roman Catholics who are seeking to retain some of their worship and witness practices, while some others are composed of persons committed to metaphysical Christianity (including holistic health emphases and the spirituality of death and dying).

Organization

Structure and staff are kept to a minimum. There is an Annual Conference to which each member unit may send two voting delegates, both of whom may be laity, but only one may be clergy. At this conference statements of concern on social problems are voted for reference to member units, decisions made regarding Council membership in wider ecumenical organizations, and budget, officers and constitutional matters voted. A Board of Trustees has interim powers and employs the executive director and any assistants. Other workers are volunteer. In addition to the Board, there are elected commissions, appointed committees, and four auxiliaries (woman, men, young adults, and youth) whose presidents serve on the Board. The U.S.A. has three zones (Western, Central, and Eastern) with the Council president and two vice presidents serving as zonal leaders. Each zone has three regions, each with a trustee as leader.

Some regions are further divided into areas, each with an area coordinator as leader.

The Council is supported by voluntary contributions, not assessments, but giving goals are suggested and achievements noted. A unit forfeits membership if it contributes nothing during a fiscal year. Financial support from a church or center for a wider ecumenical organization is voluntary. The Council has no educational institutions or mission agencies of its own, but it endorses certain ecumenical ones, which are supported voluntarily.

Neither licensing nor ordaining clergy, the Council affirms a Community Church's licensing or ordaining, or a local church's acceptance of a denomination's licensing or ordaining. The Council is an ecclesiastical endorsing agent of the U.S. government. A Community Church cleric is not required to terminate his or her denominational standing. To quote Orvis F. Jordan again:

> ...a Community Church may be described as a congregation in which denominational loyalties have been made subservient to the local religious program, and in which Christianity is thought of as involving a program of character-building and community service. A Community Church, being adjusted to the needs of the community it serves, must be different in detail in every different community.

Worship

According to J. Philip Smith, moderator of the Council's Faith and Order Commission:

> Most Community Church congregations have incorporated a variety of customs from the rich array of the Judeo-Christian heritage. Such flexibility means variety in interpretation. But the very variety we represent is a major characteristic of the ways in which we understand our common faith. We believe that God loves all and excludes

none. We believe worship takes hold of our lives regardless of specific interpretation. So we accept the pluralism of various traditions, not as obstacles to overcome, but as gifts to celebrate.

Ecumenical Involvement

The Council seeks a "unitive, but not uniformitive, religion" in its immediate geographic area and in ever-widening circles throughout the world. It became a member of the World Council of Churches in 1974, the Consultation on Church Union in 1976, and the National Council of Churches in 1977. According to the Council's constitution:

The Council approaches the task of the church in terms of the community's need. Believing that a united community requires a united church, the movement is committed to Christian unity and works toward a united church, a church as comprehensive as the spirit and teachings of Christ and as inclusive as the love of God.

As one Council-endorsed statement puts it:

A Community Church is a spirit — and who can adequately define a spirit? It must be experienced. The basis of a Community Church is an attitude. It is an openness which does not set boundaries for investigation or expression. It neither solicits some majority opinion nor rejects any minority conviction. It works to achieve a unity of spirit while, at the same time, striving to express the spirit of unity. Sincerely believing that the basic tenets Christians hold in common are far more positive, unifying and effective than those that would tend to divide, members of a Community Church agree to differ, resolve to love, unite to serve.

UNITED CHURCH OF CHRIST

The United Church of Christ takes the word "United" in its name with utmost seriousness. The church is not only an amalgam of several previous unions, but it continues to reach out in search of unity and active ecumenical involvement. In one sense this church is only thirty-some years old — having achieved the unity of Evangelical and Reformed Churches with the Congregational Christian Churches at Cleveland, Ohio, in 1957. In another, it is as old as the Reformation and, indeed, the early apostolic church. Historically, it brings together all or a significant portion of the Evangelical Synod of North America, the Reformed Church in the United States, the Hungarian Reformed Church, the Congregational Churches, and the Christian Church.

Prior to the 1957 union into the United Church of Christ, the Evangelical Synod of North America (a nineteenth-century German-American church of the frontier Mississippi Valley) and the Reformed Church in the United States (Swiss-German churches in Pennsylvania and neighboring colonies that became a Synod in 1793) had united in 1934 to form the Evangelical and Reformed Church. Their forerunners in Europe were largely Pietists from the states of Germany who had sought release from the desolations of the Thirty Years' War and the Peace of Westphalia (1648) by moving first to England, then to the American colonies. When Hungary was reclaimed by

Catholicism, many Hungarian Reformed Christians emigrated to America, and their church joined the Reformed Church in the U.S. in 1921. The Calvin Synod of the present UCC is composed of forty Hungarian congregations. Two of the best-known twentieth-century theologians, the brothers H. Richard and Reinhold Niebuhr, were nurtured in the Evangelical Church with its German rootage.

The other stream that came together as the United Church of Christ was a confluence of Congregational Churches and the Christian Church. The Congregationalists were reformists and dissenters of the Church of England, some of whom fled persecution to Holland and came as Pilgrims aboard the *Mayflower* in 1620 to the New World. Others, like leader John Winthrop, came directly from England to form the Massachusetts Bay Colony. Early New England history is inextricably interwoven with Puritan Congregationalism and Presbyterian Reformers. John Cotton, Cotton Mather, Thomas Hooker (regarded by many as the "father of democracy" in America through his less restrictive Connecticut Colony policies that were embedded in the U.S. Constitution), John Eliot (missionary to Native Americans), and Jonathan Edwards are just a few of the stars in this remarkable era of early American Congregationalism.

Meanwhile, the Second Great Awakening combined with the American frontier spirit to stir among many diverse congregations (Baptist, Methodist, Presbyterian) a desire for simplicity, unity, and a non-episcopal governance among those churches with bishops. Gradually these churches found one another, and a movement called the "Christian Connection" was organized in 1820. The Civil War painfully divided them until 1890. A group of ex-slaves formed its own conferences, which met in 1892 as the Afro-American Convention. In 1931 representatives of the Christian Church gathered in Seattle, Washington, to unite with the Congregational Churches.

The concept of congregationalism, with its emphasis upon the autonomy and individuality of each local congregation, sometimes functioned more as hindrance than help toward unity. Both Douglas Horton and Truman B. Douglass, leaders in the formation of the United Church of Christ, argued that Christ's Headship and the "priesthood of all believers" evoked both autonomy and fellowship, and that neither local church nor denominational governing body was to be subordinate to the other. Some Congregationalists resisted the union and became the National Association of Congregational Christian Churches.

Major Doctrines

Deep grounding in biblical theology binds these disparate traditions together. A trinitarian "Statement of Faith" was approved by the General Synod in 1959, and an inclusive language version was later approved by the Executive Council in 1981. Although such unity is achieved by not requiring adherence to specific creeds, three theological statements of the Reformation (Augsburg Confession, Luther's Catechism and the Heidelberg Catechism) formed the basis of the Evangelical Synod's doctrine, and Calvin and Zwingli influenced the Reformed Church (German and Swiss).

Thirty years after its formation, the United Church of Christ is engaged in serious theological debate and self-examination. Four recent statements are indicative of this struggle for theological self-understanding: an appeal in 1983 signed by thirty-nine theologians and teachers ("A Most Difficult and Urgent Time"), a letter emerging from the 1984 Craigville Colloquy, the 1983 Dubuque Declaration (Biblical Witness Fellowship), and the 1985 paper "The Prophet Speaks to Our time," prepared by Christians for Justice Action. Clyde Steckel summarized in reflections for the NCC Commission on Faith and Order:

Lutheran, Calvinist, Pietist, and Puritan strands of theology; New England, Frontier, German and German-Russian, and some Armenian ethnic strains; congregational and connectional polities are all part of the UCC inheritance. This diversity, coupled with open acceptance of recent members who increasingly claim their own agendas, make for much current theological ferment.

Geography

With 1.7 million members and 6,400-plus congregations, the UCC is predominantly White, but many congregations are ethnically and racially mixed, while some are almost entirely African-American, Armenian, Asian and Pacific Islander, Hispanic, Hungarian or Native American. Congregational roots remain strong in New England, while the Christian Churches remain influential in North Carolina and Kentucky. German churches founded along the Eastern seaboard and the Midwest continue to feed into the United Church. A recent mapping of UCC membership shows that 71 percent of all UCC members live in the northeast quadrant of the U.S. and east of the Mississippi River; at the opposite side of the country there is numerical strength in California, with very modest numbers of congregations between.

Organization

A decentralized, "free church" governance characterizes the UCC. There are no bishops or presbyters. Authority lies with each congregation, which belongs to an area organization called an association, or, if there is no association, directly to a regional conference. The highest deliberative body is the biennial General Synod, whose 700 delegates are named from the conferences, and a forty-three-member Executive Council that acts as the General Synod between sessions. General Synod approves budgets, elects officers, maintains the treasury, adopts and amends the constitution and bylaws, and determines ecumenical relationships; its resolutions and social/theological stands are not binding on local churches or individual members, but do bear the authority of a covenantal relationship. The UCC structure has two mission boards (homeland and world ministries), pension boards, a foundation, and six other national bodies that provide leadership and program, especially in social issues and public policy advocacy.

Worship

The style of worship among the congregations in the United Church of Christ varies greatly, as befits the varied traditions that are represented in this ecumenical church. Some worship is relatively formal; other churches are freer, more spontaneous, such as in the tradition of the Black churches. Some congregations regularly use the Statement of Faith, while others recite early historic creeds, and still others choose not to use creeds in worship. The UCCs have recently produced a much-commended Book of Worship that reflects the attempts to be inclusive in church traditions, in racial and ethnic cultural material, and through non-sexist language.

The UCC heritage includes the first ordination of a woman in the United States — the Rev. Antoinette Brown, who was ordained as minister of the Congregational Church of South Butler, New York, in 1853. Baptism and Communion, or Eucharist, are the two sacraments recognized in the United Church of Christ. More congregations tend to use infant Baptism than adult believer's Baptism by immersion. No single doctrine on the nature of Christ's presence in the elements of Communion is required for membership or participation. True worship involves being illumined and renewed in covenantal relationship through the Holy Spirit's guidance in the reading and preaching of Scripture. Commitment to transformation of human society toward the Kingdom of God is necessary to be fully rather than minimally Christian.

Ecumenical Involvement

A "united and uniting church," the United Church of Christ is a member of the National and World Councils of Churches and is a participant in the Consultation on Church Union. Under the unique "Plan of Union" of 1801, both Congregationalists and Presbyterians worked together so closely in their missionary efforts that a pastor could serve either church. This lasted until 1852. Today the Christian Church (Disciples of Christ), which itself came into existence through the yearning for unity, and the United Church are in "ecumenical partnership" to engage in a number of programs and activities together. A delegation of the United Church of Christ led in 1976 by their president, Robert V. Moss, Jr., visited four United Churches in other nations in recognition of common historic missionary roots. More recently

the United Church of Christ has formalized partner relation-
ships with the Evangelical Church of the Union in German, the
Presbyterian Church, Republic of Korea, and the Pentecostal
Church of Chile.

THE UNITED METHODIST CHURCH

John Wesley did not intend to found a new church. A firm believer in the universal church, his doctrine of the church included appreciation for the Catholic understanding of tradition and the Eucharist, Reformation doctrines on Scripture, preaching, and the priesthood of all believers, and the Pietist's emphasis on discipleship and radical commitment. He and his brother Charles took their reforming interest in a holy society within the Church of England from their Oxford group to the American colonies, where they were influenced by the Moravians. The Georgia colony proving to be somewhat daunting, John returned in 1738 to England, where he had his "Aldersgate" spirit-warmed experience. Reinvigorated, he established the distinctive United Societies of the People Called Methodists and soon was sending missionary preachers to the American colonies, where lay preachers had already begun to spread Methodism.

In colonial America the religious landscape was far different from England, where the Church of England was dominant. The pluralism of religious life, the frontier style of impatient and independent American church leaders, the necessity of defining the Episcopal role as well as that of Methodism, the inaction of the Anglicans, the powerful forces of revivalism, and the equivocal role of John Wesley all played a part in the formation of the Methodist society as a church. Although no official minutes have survived, a gathering of preachers, including Thomas

Coke, fresh from visiting John Wesley in England, and the rigorous Francis Asbury, met in a chapel on Lovely Lane in Baltimore on Christmas Eve, 1784, to form the Methodist Episcopal Church.

While Methodist preachers were itinerating into the expanding borders of the newly-established United States of America, a group of pastors from the Mennonite and the German Reformed Church, highly influenced by Wesley and Asbury, organized the United Brethren Church in 1800. Sometimes called the "German Methodists," their leaders, such as William Otterbein and Martin and Henry Boehm, sought to imitate Methodist polity and discipline. Because they elected bishops for four-year terms and allowed both traveling and local preachers voting rights in annual conferences, they maintained their separateness from the Methodists.

Three years after the gathering of United Brethren, Jacob Albright, a self-taught and deeply committed Methodist itinerating preacher, convened his helpers to form a society that was the beginning of the Evangelical Association. Both of these groups reflected the Pietist tradition and valued personal religious experience, tending to avoid controversial political and social issues. The Evangelical Association maintained its firm devotion to German language and tradition and resisted for over 150 years becoming a church by holding to the Pietistic concept of "ecclesiola in ecclesia." Only in 1946 did they and the United Evangelicals, with whom they had mended a schism in 1922, join with the United Brethren Church to form the Evangelical United Brethren Church.

Black Christians from the very outset had been attracted to Methodism. Racism that racked the nation also affected the Methodist Episcopal Church, however. The John Street Church in New York City, which began by buying the freedom of Peter Williams, sexton (who insisted upon paying them back), later became the congregation from which the African Methodist Episcopal Zion Church emerged. The African Methodist Episcopal Church began with the Richard Allen-led walkout from St. George's in Philadelphia over segregated seating. But Black presence also remained within the Methodist Episcopal Church, and Black pastors down through the years who maintained fellowship with White Christians are as much leaders of the "Black Church" as those who left.

Before the Civil War the Methodist Episcopal Church, South was formed over a specific complex controversy concerning the ownership of slaves, and differences in governance kept them apart from the Methodist Episcopal Church, North until 1939. During the time of separation the Christian (originally Colored) Methodist Episcopal Church was formed with the blessing of the Methodist Episcopal Church, South.

By the twentieth century a number of changes in Methodism had taken place. The stringent but effective policy of itinerating ministry was being modified. The small group approach, called "classes," was no longer needed with more pastors being "located." Worship was becoming more structured and ministers were being educated through courses of study and theological schools.

Today a Methodist theology that stressed the dignity and equality of individuals can be appreciated as hospitable to and an effective grounding for American democracy. Its concern for perfection in individuals (sanctification) and betterment of society has put it in the forefront of issues like temperance and use of tobacco, justice for women and minorities, labor relations, and world hunger and poverty. Methodism continues to struggle with a tension between authoritarian direction and democratic self-government.

The Evangelical United Brethren, itself a merger, and the Methodist Church that reunited the "Northern" and "Southern" Methodist Episcopal Churches and the Methodist Protestant Church in 1939 came together in Dallas in 1968 to form the United Methodist Church.

Major Doctrines
The theological roots of Methodism are in John Wesley's thought, which emphasizes the traditional sources of religious knowledge: Scripture, the Tradition, reason, and experience. Affirming his Catholic and Anglican heritage, Wesley took the normative authority of the early church, the importance of the

sacraments, and the contribution of the Eastern Fathers very se-
riously. Distinct contributions to theology are the concept of
prevenient grace (the grace that "comes before" the turn toward
salvation), the assurance that one is on the road to salvation,
and the lifelong process of going on to perfection.

Geography

Thanks to the efforts of a travelling ministry and broad appeal, Methodism is located in strength all over the United States.
It is truly an "American Church." But through the unique organization into "conferences," described below, it is also very
international. In 1985 the United Methodist Church membership totalled 9,182,172 in the U.S., plus Central Conferences
in Africa, Europe and the Philippines. These "Central Conferences," most often products of American missionary work,
are Annual Conferences that sought to be more self-determining
than being "missionary conferences" allowed them to be, while
at the same time maintaining their organic relationship with the
United Methodist Church. Their units of organization are every
bit as "United Methodist" as is the Minnesota Conference or
the Texas Conference. Some Central Conferences sought even
more independence from the United Methodist Church and during the last century became autonomous Methodist Churches in
their own countries, while maintaining affiliation with their parent body.

Both British and American Methodists have had an active
world mission program that is strong in many parts of the world,
but has been particularly formative in India, Africa and the Far
East.

Organization

A quadrennial General Conference of clergy and laity is the
authoritative legislative body, but there is also an often critically
important Judicial Council. The Council of Bishops has the key
responsibility for spiritual and temporal affairs of the communion. Jurisdictional conferences elect bishops, and within the
jurisdictions are annual conferences, which have district super-

intendents. At the local church level a charge conference meets at least twice annually to conduct the local church's business. Women, including temperance and women's rights leader Frances Willard, have played many important roles in the church. The first female preacher, Margaret Van Cott, was licensed in 1866, and Amanda Smith, a Black slave washerwoman became world famous as an evangelist, although women lay delegates to the General Conference were not allowed until 1892. United Methodists are committed to the ordination of women and have, since 1980, elected three bishops who were women. By 1988 nearly forty women served as district superintendents and almost 2,000 women were fully ordained and serving in local churches.

Worship

The sermon remains central to Methodist worship, although worship has evolved from a revival-type free-flowing spontaneity to a more structured kind of service, signalled by the publication of *The Methodist Hymnal* in 1836. John Wesley had intended the American Methodists to use his revision of the Anglican *Book of Common Prayer*, but this never received acceptance. Love feasts and the watchnight "Covenant Service" have been important in Wesleyan worship, and the hymns of Charles Wesley symbolize the importance of singing Methodist theology. Because of the scarcity of ordained elders in earlier times, the Lord's Supper in the American church was usually celebrated quarterly.

Ecumenical Involvement

Through the years both Wesleyan theology and Methodist Church action have marked the United Methodists as strongly ecumenical in spirit. Methodists are active in the National and World Council of Churches, the Consultation on Church Union, and the Joint Strategy and Action Committee. In 1964 they established a denominational ecumenical office and have provided strong leadership and funds to the ecumenical movement. The World Methodist Council brings over sixty churches in more than ninety countries into association. A regular quadrennial meeting of bishops and other leaders has forged new relationships between the historic Black churches and the United Methodist Church. United Methodists honor diversity, seek responsible participation of clergy and lay, male and female, ethnic and racial minorities, strive toward a life of devotion undergirding activism, and look for the things that unite the children of God.

3

AFRICAN-AMERICAN
CHURCHES

AFRICAN METHODIST EPISCOPAL CHURCH

A tablet on the front porch of a two-story log dwelling in the Pipe Creek Settlement south of New Windsor, Maryland, declares that this is "the birthplace of American Methodism" as well as the home of Robert Strawbridge, who formed the first Methodist society. Other key figures in the rise of Methodism are Francis Asbury and Philip Embury.

Growth of Black membership was swift, and by 1793 nearly 40 percent of American Methodists were Black. Cecil Cone says that Africans already had a concept of God as creator and God as one, and that a deeply religious outlook pervaded their lives. Thus there was a receptivity to Christianity despite the failure of many White people to be transformed by its message in their attitudes toward slavery.

This failure to recognize that "God is no respecter of persons" came to sharp focus in 1787 for Richard Allen, who, being forced in the middle of prayer to move to the balcony of St. George's Methodist Episcopal Church in Philadelphia, led his people out, later to establish Bethel Chapel, now the mother church of the African Methodist Episcopal Church. Francis Asbury dedicated the chapel and ordained Richard Allen, a former slave later to become bishop. In 1816 the African Methodist Episcopal Church was formally organized. The African Methodist Episcopal Church had tried to remain affiliated with the General Conference of the Methodist Episcopal Church, which was composed of White ministers and bishops, but concern over free exercise of control over their own property led them to form an independent organization with its own trustees.

A few further details concerning Bishop Allen enliven this brief summary. Richard Allen bought his freedom at the age of seventeen by cutting and selling cord wood to earn the staggering sum of $2,000 in continental money. Before founding the Bethel Church, he began the "Free African Society," whose program was to preach, feed the hungry, cloth the naked, house the homeless, cheer the fallen, provide jobs, minister to needs of the sick and imprisoned, and to encourage thrift and economic advancement. Leaving the society to found the Bethel Church, he worked as a shoemaker and chimney sweep to buy the building. The courts upheld the right of his church to refuse to admit an elder from St. George's Church to its pulpit, and later in that year, 1816, the AME held a convention to make it a connectional church. True to his own precepts, he taught the Bethel Church to acquire property and died with an estate valued at $40,000, a remarkable amount for any American and particularly for a Black man of his time.

Charles Wesley said of Richard Allen at his death in 1831:

> He was the first Negro in the modern world to gain the office of Bishop in any branch of the Christian Church in the U.S., the organizer of the oldest nationally independent Negro church on American soil, and a leader in the development of organized cooperative Negro life. He taught the Negroes of America a lesson in self-help, not in oratory alone, but in monuments of brick and stone, in deeds and accomplishments which are the admiration of those who love liberty and the defense of manhood's privileges.

Today's language would say it differently, but the message is clear.

Major Doctrines

Although Methodism adopted to varying degrees the doctrinal standards of its founder, John Wesley, there has always been latitude to experience God's love in a personal and individual way and to receive the saving grace of Christ. The AMEs have emphasized dignity and respect for personality. Beginning with Richard Allen, they have strongly linked the Christian faith to concern for poverty and the struggle for economic and social justice. A dominating theme for Allen's theology was God's election and the empowerment of an oppressed people to struggle for justice in society.

Although the concept of Black theology is not uniformly understood or accepted within the AME Church, its first clear exponent is Prof. James Cone, AME theologian at Union Theological Seminary in New York City. It is a major contribution to current theological thinking in churches around the world.

Geography

Although the AME Church was founded in the North and flourished there, its membership increased rapidly in the South after the Civil War, and today it is found all across the nation. Its numbers are estimated at roughly 2.5 million.

Organization

There are nineteen districts, most of which have bishops; and a General Conference is held quadrennially (the last was 1988). A General Board holds an annual meeting, and the Council of Bishops also meets annually. There are fourteen departments headed by persons located around the nation. Officers include the general secretary, senior bishop, the presidents and secretaries of the Council of Bishops and the General Board, the treasurer, historiographer, and the president of the Judicial Council.

Worship

As AME theologian James Cone says,

Black worship is essentially a spiritual experience of the truth of Black life. The experience is spiritual because the people encounter the presence of the holy spirit in their midst. Black worship is truthful because the spirit's presence authenticates their experience of freedom by empow-

ering them with courage and strength to bear witness in
their present existence to what they know is coming in
God's own eschatological future.

Worship strongly emphasizes preaching, prayer, and communal
fellowship more than liturgy; and music ranging from Gospel
hymns and spirituals to classical music is an important ingredi-
ent.

James Cone lists six elements of Black worship: preaching,
singing, shouting, conversion, prayer, and testimony, because
"it is the people's response to the presence of the spirit that
creates the unique style of Black worship." They respond with
joy "when God's Spirit visits their worship and stamps a new
identity upon their personhood in contrast to their oppressed
status in White society." Likewise, Black prayer is an event to
be experienced, which is as important as the words being spoken,
and worship is "the actualization of the story of salvation."

Ecumenical Involvement

The AME Church is a member of both the World and National Councils of Churches, is a participant in the Consultation on Church Union, and is a cooperating denomination in
the Joint Strategy and Action Committee. It also participates in
the Congress of National Black Churches. AME Bishop Philip
R. Cousin was the first president (1984–1987) of the National
Council of Churches of Christ in the U.S.A. from one of the
historic Black churches.

AFRICAN METHODIST EPISCOPAL ZION CHURCH

Like the AME Church and at nearly the same time, the founders of the AME Zion Church, who had been part of the Methodist Episcopal Church in the early days and beginnings of the United States of America, withdrew to assert their own leadership.

James Varick, son of a slave woman and a Dutch slaveholder, was influenced by the Methodist ministry of Philip Embury and joined the John Street Methodist Episcopal Church, from which he became licensed to preach. In 1796 he and thirty others, disturbed by segregated seating and other slights, departed to form the first Black church of New York, now known as the Mother AME Zion Church and located on West 137th Street in New York City, after moving from several other locations in the city.

Soon named its first bishop, Varick led the expansion of the AME Zion Church into forming a communion, and a formal discipline was drawn up in 1820. Varick also pioneered in helping to start the first Black newspaper in New York State, *Freedom's Journal*. Known as the "anti-slavery" church for its particularly strong itineration of preachers for abolition, the AME Zion Church counts Harriet Tubman, Sojourner Truth, Katherine Harris and Frederick Douglass as key figures in its history. "A sort of pertinacity was bred into these women who stood by the side of the men, fought the battles of freedom, and expanded the church across the continent and across the seas," notes historian Bishop William J. Walls of numerous AME Zion women who, from its earliest existence, played a vigorous role. One of them, Mary Roberts of the Mother AME Zion Church, organized the Daughters of Conference and presided over it for over forty years. This organization helped establish churches and was active in both home and international missions. In 1880 the Woman's Home and Foreign Missionary Society was founded, which is vigorous to this day, its name having been changed in 1980 to the Woman's Home and *Overseas* Missionary Society.

Like other Black churches emerging out of the injustices and humiliation of slavery, the AMEZ Church has been, in Gunnar Myrdal's judgment, "a giver of hope, an emotional cathartic, a center of community activity, a source of leadership, and a provider of respectability." Through the Black church an organized social existence beyond the family was possible, political life could be nurtured, educational hopes addressed, and a public dialogue encouraged. Publications like *The Star of Zion* and the *AME Zion Quarterly Review* and such schools as Livingstone College and Clinton Junior College are outgrowths of these large purposes.

During their formative years, the AME Zion congregations met with AME leaders from Philadelphia with some hope of making common cause, since Bishop Allen had already taken a firm stand with the Methodist Episcopal Church. Zion Methodists were more oriented toward a strong laity and at first did not elect bishops, but superintendents, to places of leadership in the newly-forming structure. The Bethel leaders were following a more traditional episcopal form of church government and expected the AME Zion leaders to adapt within it. Although a way was not found to bring the New York and Philadelphia African Methodists together in those early years, there have been repeated efforts throughout the century following to do so. As of 1986 the AME Zion Church is engaged in merger negotiations with another Methodist Church, the Christian Methodist Episcopal Church, also grown from the same Methodist Episcopal

Church roots. In 1848 the AME Zion Church chose its present name.

Major Doctrines

With a background in Wesley Methodism, the AME Zion Church has expressed itself theologically as it struggled over the Gospel's assurances of dignity, hope, and salvation through the love of Christ and the surrounding realities of slavery and oppression. Louis Lomax makes the point that the key terms of Christian faith — salvation, freedom, Kingdom of God, etc. — carry different meaning to the imagery than that of Whites. Sadness mingles with joy, and hope rises in special identification with the release of the Israelites from bondage in Egypt, as Blacks sing their own version of "Let my People Go."

The Apostles' Creed is the only formal creed, and the articles of religion, discipline, and constitutional requirements are shared with the Methodist Episcopal heritage. Other prominent doctrinal themes are: sanctification, the witness of the Spirit, the life of joy and obedience following repentance, Christian experience, means of grace, and conversion.

Geography

The AME Zion Church is far stronger east of the Mississippi than beyond it, and it spread rapidly throughout the northern states as well as into the southeast, with particular concentration in North Carolina. Its membership is estimated at 1.5 million, located on five continents.

Organization

There are twelve episcopal areas, each with a bishop. There is an Annual Conference at which the presiding bishop makes assignments, and District Conferences headed by a presiding elder. There are eleven departments, a publishing house, a Connectional Lay Council, and the Woman's Home and Overseas Missionary Society. Missionaries have been sent to several African countries, South America, and the West Indies. A central form of church polity governs each congregation as part of the denomination, while each congregation maintains its own distinct identity. Every four years there is a General Conference, the last held in Charlotte in 1988.

Worship

Methodist worship emphasizes simplicity in buildings and dress. W. E. B. DuBois speaks of three gifts: a gift of story and song ("soft, stirring melody in an ill-harmonized and unmelodious land"), the gift of sweat and brawn, and the gift of the Spirit. "...Out of the nations' heart we have called all that was best to throttle and subdue all that was worst: Fire and blood, prayer and sacrifice, have billowed over this people, and they have found peace only in the altars of the God of Right," claimed DuBois. Family worship is also stressed, as is the ritual recognition of occasions and milestones of life. Music is one of the special emphases. Congregational hymn singing and large choirs show the vitality and versatility of music in Black worship life, along with "the oratory of the heart."

Ecumenical Involvement

The AME Zion Church is vigorously ecumenical, with involvement in both WCC and NCC, the World Methodist Council, Church Women United, the American Bible Society, the Consultation on Church Union, the Congress of National Black Churches, and is a cooperating denomination of the Joint Strategy and Action Committee. It also continues to examine the fruitful possibilities of bringing together the Black Methodist Episcopal churches, with special attention currently to a merger plan with the Christian Methodist Episcopal Church.

CHRISTIAN METHODIST EPISCOPAL CHURCH

The Christian Methodist Episcopal Church, or the CME as it is commonly called, arose in the aftermath of the Civil War and the problems of the Reconstruction Era as Black Christians who had been slave members of the Methodist Episcopal Church, South, desired their own separate and independent religious organization. It was organized December 16, 1870, in Jackson, Tennessee, as the Colored Methodist Episcopal Church in America. By 1930, the "in America" had dropped from the name, and in 1954, the racial designation, "Colored," was replaced by the term "Christian."

The organization and history of the Christian Methodist Episcopal Church is a unique example of what might be termed the institutionalization of the Black religious experience. Randall Albert Carter, one of the more influential leaders in an earlier period of the CME Church, described the motivation that prompted the early "Colored Methodists" to establish their own denomination this way:

They wanted to try the experiment of making a church of colored people who, though but yesterday slaves, would work and live in the territory which was then owned and controlled by their former masters. In that little band of pioneers were men who were destined to leave their impress

indelibly upon the thought of coming generations. Think
you of the afflictions, necessities, distresses, tumults, jour-
neyings often ... hunger and thirst, fastings often, cold and
nakedness which would be theirs, as they sought to foster
and nourish this tender plant of God.

This means that in the main, the religious experience of those
who would organize the CME Church, as it was with the origins of virtually all of the independent Black churches in America, was grounded in the slavery experience in which all Black
Americans share. But slave religion was devoid of effective institutional development — it had "preaching," "singing," and
"shouting," but no responsibility for its support or its contin-
uation. After emancipation, the religion of the slaves required
institutional development. That development of necessity had
to be apart from the institutions of the White churches out of
which the religion itself had sprung. Thus, the Black church is a
paradox of the spiritual continuity with Protestant Christianity
but a radical discontinuity with the organizational structures of
Protestant Christianity. The CME Church exemplifies this con-
tinuity/discontinuity paradox in its historical relationship with
the Methodist Episcopal Church, South.

The CME Church also exemplifies an amicable relationship
with the "parent" religious body out of which it came. It is
the only Black Methodist body organized with the full coop-
eration, along with the legal and ecclesiastical authority, of the
White denomination that gave it birth. The Organizing General
Conference of the CME Church was authorized by the General
Conference of the Methodist Episcopal Church, South. The first
bishops elected by the CME Church — William Henry Miles of
Kentucky and Richard H. Vanderhorst of Georgia — were ordained by Bishop Robert Paine and Bishop H. N. McTyeire of
the M. E. Church, South; and all the properties that had been
used for the slave members were authorized to be deeded to the
new CME Church. Throughout its history, the CME Church has
been strongly supported by the M. E. Church, South, as might
be seen in the joint sponsorship of Paine College in Augusta,
Georgia.

The name "Methodist Episcopal Church, *South*" itself requires explanation in the history of American Methodism, however. In 1844 the Fifteenth Session of the General Conference of the Methodist Episcopal Church met in New York, and embarrassment arose over the fact that, through inheritance and marriage, Bishop James O. Andrew had become a slave owner, and the General Conference voted that he desist from exercising his office "so long as this impediment remains." Southern delegates protested, and a plan of separation into two churches was proposed and adopted by the General Conference.

The history of the Christian Methodist Episcopal Church, according to Bishop Othal Hawthorne Lakey in *The History of the CME Church* (1985), "shares in God's history, the history of salvation, the history that continues. It shares in God's history because through it all . . . the Gospel of Jesus Christ was preached and the sacrament duly administered, thousands of souls were saved, the sick visited and cared for, the dead were buried, the bereaved were comforted, the hungry were fed, the ignorant were taught, broken hearts were healed, faith was strengthened, hope was found, and righteousness proclaimed!"

Major Doctrines

The doctrinal emphases of the CME Church coincide with Protestant Christianity generally and those of Wesleyan Methodism specifically — the twenty-five Articles of Religion of American Methodism being the literal statement of its doctrines, and the Apostles' Creed and the Nicene Creed being its creedal expression. In its practical application of doctrine, the CME Church has placed emphasis on social justice and human inclusiveness, recognizing the rights of all persons to be members of the church.

Geography

As this history makes clear, the CMEs are mostly strong in the South, with one district on the West Coast. Dramatic shifts caused by Black migration from the rural South to the urban North and urban South beginning around 1930 have affected the CME membership, especially certain conferences. By 1960, the CMEs had a majority of members in the rural South, but had also become an urban denomination with its largest congregations in the cities and composed of Black middle-class members. Its inclusive membership is over 700,000, with mission conferences in Nigeria, Ghana, Liberia, Haiti, and Jamaica.

Organization

The CME Church follows the "conference" structure of historic Methodism, with a quadrennial General Conference having full power to make the rules and regulations for the church, an Annual Conference of which the ordained clergy are members and to which representatives from local congregations are representatives, and Quarterly and Church Conferences, which oversee the operation of the local churches. The CME Church is an "Episcopal" church in that its ecclesiastical authority is vested in bishops who are the spiritual and moral leaders of the denomination with exclusive powers to appoint pastors to local congregations. The bishops preside over episcopal districts, which are geographical entities, nine of which are in the continental United States, while a tenth constitutes CME missions in Africa.

The administrative programs of the CME Church are through various departments that are related to the life and witness of the church, each governed by a departmental board and administered by a general secretary. The most influential of such departments is the Women's Missionary Council, which arose, ironically, as a result of the denial of women's rights to participate fully in the life of the church in its early history. Today, women are granted full rights of ministry in the church; many women serve successfully as pastors, and one serves as a presiding elder.

Worship

The worship of the Christian Methodist Episcopal Church is, for the most part, traditional Black worship with a strong emphasis on preaching, singing, prayer, reciting the creed, responsive Scriptures, and a formal ritual for the observance of Holy Communion. Generally, worship in CME congregations has a very strong emotional overtone and bespeaks the ethos of what has been described as "soul." In keeping with the Black religious style, the role of the Black preacher is paramount both in the service of worship and preaching, but also in the administration of the church and in community leadership.

Ecumenical Involvement

The CME Church has been in the forefront of ecumenical developments from very early in its history. There was representation at the first "ecumenical" conference in London in 1881 (an "all Methodist" event). The first gathering of Christian churches in what later became the Federation of Churches had a strong CME delegation. The Federated Council of Bishops — an organization of bishops of Black Methodist bodies — led to a strong attempt to unite the three major Black Methodist bodies in 1918, and though the CME Church strongly opposed the actual union, its bishops were most active in that council. The organization of the National Council of Churches and the World Council of Churches had active CME involvement. Bishop B. Julian Smith was a renowned ecumenist. Presently, the CME Church is engaged in serious union negotiations with the African Methodist Episcopal Zion Church.

NATIONAL BAPTIST CONVENTION
IN AMERICA

Baptists readily trace themselves back to John the Baptist, Christ's public ministry, and to Pentecost, but their distinct historical contribution is linked with the Separatist movement in England near the end of the sixteenth century. Some historians also find an influence upon the English Baptists from the Mennonites during the English exile in the Netherlands, although not all Mennonite theology was accepted by the English refugees.

In any case, the National Baptist Convention in America owes its own existence, since 1915, most directly to the twenty-year older National Baptist Convention of America, organized in Atlanta in 1895. Because of the dispute over the ultimate control of a burgeoning publishing house, the Convention addressed the issue by drawing up a charter of incorporation. Those who sided with the Publishing Board rejected the charter and withdrew to form the National Baptist Convention in America, thus sometimes referred to as the "unincorporated" body. There are no doctrinal or other major differences between the two National Baptist Conventions and the original divisive issue has receded in importance.

Although the first Black Baptist church was organized in South Carolina in 1773, the rapid growth of Black Baptist congregations occurred after the Civil War. White slaveholders had sometimes encouraged the teaching of Christianity to their slaves, but the slave rebellion led by Black Baptist Nat Turner in Virginia in 1831 brought increased resistance to the preaching activity of free Blacks, separate assembly by Black congregations, and literacy among the slaves. The Great Awakening had brought revival preaching that, while carefully avoiding the subject of slavery itself, had revolutionary implications of equality: "The blessed Savior died and shed his blood as much for you as for your master, or any of the White people.... He has opened the door of heaven wide for you and invites you all to enter," said the itinerant preacher. Revivalist Protestant Christianity became, according to Sydney Ahlstrom and E. Franklin Frazier, the chief means by which the African slave — bereft of his own culture, language, and religion — defined and explained his or her personal and social existence in America. Or, as W. E. B. DuBois states it, "A proscribed people must have a social center, and that center for this people is the Negro Church."

Twentieth-century Black Baptists have faced challenges different from the move from slavery to freedom, but by no means of minor significance. Accused by sociologist E. Franklin Frazier of making the Black church "the most important barrier to integration and the assimilation of members" into the larger society, the Black churches have come to see the virtue in that very accusation, as they recognize their role in preserving the Afro-American heritage and Black solidarity. The huge migration to the urban centers of America after World War I upset the pattern of nearly 90 percent of U.S. Blacks living in the South, two-thirds of whom were in rural settings. By 1965, 75 percent of Black Americans were living in cities, about half in the urban North. An entire way of life, the moral and spiritual as well as the social and economic, was disruptively transformed, and the Black churches have borne a heavy burden in this upheaval, including the diminishment of their own authority in the secularized city.

Ever since emancipation, Black clergy have had to choose whether to side with a Garvey-type "back to Africa" movement and its more recent version in Malcolm X's Black nationalism, the faithful unresentfulness of Booker T. Washington that makes the best of political inequality and social segregation, or various degrees of Black Power and the Civil Rights movement typified by William E. B. DuBois and Martin Luther King. Like theologian James H. Cone, many Black Baptist clergy have found the Gospel of Jesus Christ consistent with Black Power, providing it an ethical basis and an identification with the world's oppressed.

Major Doctrines

The basic Baptist tenets of Christ's authority over one's life and the individual's ability to discern religious truth in relation to God hold for the NBC of America. As with other Black Baptists, however, the separation of church and state issue is handled somewhat differently from White Baptist churches. The church has been the social center of the Black community, including its political life. Involvement in the larger society has been a matter of serious theological debate as well as of precarious and tenuous political power, so that pragmatically the churches have led both in citizen education and partisan politics.

Geography

The second largest group of Black Baptists, the NBCA has been estimated to have as many as 3.5 million members across the country. A focal point of its ministry is the National Baptist Convention of America Publishing Board in Nashville, Tennessee. A significant project is the annual National Baptist Sunday School and Training Union Congress and a major printing plant. Missions are conducted in Liberia, Jamaica, Panama, the West Indies and the Bahama Islands.

Organization

The officers are president, corresponding secretary, treasurer, historian and a statistician. There are four major boards, a Baptist Training Union, Junior Mission and Senior Women's Missionary Auxiliaries (two auxiliaries for women), a National Baptist Youth Convention, a National Baptist Brotherhood, a benevolent Commission, and a National Ushers Auxiliary. There is little difference between the NBC of America and the NBCUSA in theology, but each has had strong central leadership while affirming the spiritual democracy within congregationalism.

Worship

Central themes of the faith of the Black church are justice, love, and hope. No more eloquent testimony to these themes, both in rhetoric and in life, can be found than in the Rev. Martin Luther King, Jr. He carried his personal struggle of faith into the pulpit, as he described one night of frustration and despair after a threatening telephone call. He could not sleep, went to the kitchen for a cup of coffee, and found himself drawing upon the depths of the faith of his own father:

> You've got to call on that something, on that person that your daddy used to tell you about, the power that can make a way out of no way. And I discovered then that religion had to become real to me and I had to know God for myself. And I bowed down over the cup of coffee. I never will forget it. Oh yes, I prayed a prayer. And I prayed out loud that night. I said, "Lord, I'm down here trying to do what's right. I think I'm right. I think the cause that we represent is right. But Lord, I must confess that I'm weak now, I'm faltering, I'm losing my courage, and I can't let the people see me like this because if they see me weak and losing my courage they will begin to get weak."

Then King testified to hearing a liberating inner voice that said, "Martin Luther, stand up for righteousness. Stand up for justice. Stand up for truth. And lo, I will be with you, even until the end of the world." His own personal struggle for faith became the struggle of his people, and together in worship they were encouraged to "keep on keeping on." Some Black clergy, as with some Whites, have faltered or accommodated themselves to the *status quo*, and there are Black critics of the Black church for these accommodations. But the Kings, the Gayraud Wilmores, the Anna Hedgemans, the Gardiner Taylors, the Jim Cones, the Vincent Hardings, the Fannie Lou Hamers, the Jim Forbeses and numerous other stalwarts of the faith join the early heroes as a witness to the power of worship and preaching in the Black church toward the healing of a people and of a nation.

Ecumenism

Perhaps the truest evidence of ecumenism among the Black churches is the relative difficulty one has in knowing "denominational" allegiances of outstanding Black church leaders, who transcend their labels because the faith and the struggles transcend them. The NBC in America participates as a member of the National and World Council of Churches.

NATIONAL BAPTIST CONVENTION OF THE UNITED STATES OF AMERICA, INCORPORATED

At the time of the American Revolution Baptists were the third largest Christian body in the colonies, next to Congregationalists and Presbyterians. Besides Roger Williams' organization in Rhode Island, the Baptists developed strength around Philadelphia, many of them coming from England and Wales. In 1773 at Silver Bluff, South Carolina, the first Black Baptist church in America was organized by George Leisle (Leile), a Virginia slave, and a White deacon, Wait Palmer. By 1778 Leisle had helped to organize the First African Baptist Church of Savannah, Georgia, along with convert Jesse Peters and a White pastor named Abraham Marshall. Meanwhile other churches were being organized in Virginia among the slaves. By 1793 one fourth of the 73,471 Baptists in the U.S. were Blacks, despite the ambivalence of White slaveholders about teaching religion and laws that restricted the slave's freedom of assembly. The usual practice was to compose local churches of both White and Black members, allotting Blacks special seats in the balcony, even though they often outnumbered Whites in the congregation. A number of Black preachers was also ordained during the years immediately following the American Revolution.

The Providence Baptist Association of Ohio was the first or-

ganization of Black Baptists above the local church level, begun
in 1836 and prefiguring further state level organization by about
fifty years. Meanwhile, the northern and southern largely White
Baptists were beginning to strain apart over slavery and organizational matters. In 1845 the Southern Baptist Convention was
organized, after tensions over appointment of a missionary who
was a slaveholder divided Baptist ranks, not unlike the formation of the Methodist Episcopal Church, South. After the Civil
War some 400,000 Black Baptists withdrew to organize their
own bodies. A Southern Baptist missionary to Africa, W. W.
Colley, called Black Baptists together to secure support for Black
Baptist missions in Africa. This meeting in Montgomery, Al-
abama, in 1880, resulted in the formation of the Foreign Mission
Baptist Convention. Six years later in St. Louis, the American
National Baptist Convention was organized to coordinate Black
Baptist activities, and in 1893 in the District of Columbia the
Baptist National Educational Convention was organized. These
three conventions soon saw the advantage of merger and united
into the National Baptist Convention of America at Atlanta in
1895, each major concern represented by a board.

The new Foreign Mission Board of this newly-merged body
was moved from Richmond to Louisville, a move that was dis-
tressing to Virginians and North Carolinians, and this concern,
along with several others, led to the organization of the Lott
Carey Foreign Mission Convention in 1897 in Washington, D.C.
In the next year a publishing house was begun, but unresolved
questions about ownership and control tested this newly organized convention to its breaking point. One effort to resolve
the issue, incorporation by the National Baptist Convention,
resulted in a division in 1915. Those who supported the incorporation of the Convention became known as the National
Baptist Convention of the U.S.A., Incorporated. Those who
sided with the Publishing Board established a new Convention
(National Baptist Convention in America).

Major Doctrines
The strongest uniting belief of Baptists is the basic principle
of "theological individualism" that allows for them to differ on

many other beliefs. What Roger Williams called "soul liberty" is the belief in the competency of the individual soul to interpret Christ's will for him or herself. That means that Baptists may even differ in some instances over adult Baptism and immersion. Although agreeing that it is anti-biblical to establish doctrinal unity by means of humanmade creeds and theological formulations, there are several basic tenets: the lordship of Jesus Christ and the revelation of his will in the Bible, which is the "supreme standard by which all human conduct, creeds, and opinions must be tried." Second to the basic principle is the sovereignty of the soul under God in all religious matters, the right of private judgment. The fellowship of Baptists is therefore strongest within the local congregation. Ecclesiastical structure and ecumenical relationships are approached cautiously. Baptists have brought to the concept of the priesthood of all believers a strong sense of individual responsibility for their neighbors. Black Baptists tend to be more strongly Calvinistic than some of their White counterparts.

Geography

Distributed broadly across the United States, the NBCUSA, Inc., is the largest Black Baptist convention and is parent of the others. Membership figures are estimated as high as 6.5 million, with 27,000 pastors. It operates with the Southern Baptist Convention a seminary in Nashville, the American Baptist Theological Seminary, along with several other schools and colleges of its own. There are missions in Africa, Nigeria, Nicaragua, Japan and the Bahamas.

Organization

The Convention meets annually, sometimes holding an additional adjourned session between annual meetings. Attendance at the Convention annual meeting is in the thousands from the affiliated churches. A Board of Directors handles interim business. There are six boards: foreign and home missions, Sunday school publishing, Baptist Training Union, education, and evangelism. There is a Laymen's Movement and a Woman's Auxiliary Convention, and a Congress of Christian Education. The

National Baptist Voice is published from Richmond. The officers of the Convention are a president, general secretary, several vice presidents, treasurer, statistician and historian.

Worship

One of the noted Black church pastors observes that during worship in communal fashion,

> Black people re-establish the personhood that has been brutalized during their week-long pilgrimage in White racist America. It has been the Black church, in this day as in days past, which has enabled Black people to keep the faith. It is literally as well as symbolically true that the people of the contemporary Black church still manage to "sing the Lord's song in a strange land."

As many of today's Black youth search for their Africa links, they are led to the Black church and its music. He also observes that Black churches that allowed the least tampering with their music and worship styles maintained the strongest preservation of links with an African heritage. The "mystical quality" of faith in Jesus sustains the contemporary Black church through inexpressible emotional and psychological cruelties of modern American life.

Ecumenical Involvement

Large and spread across the country with little structural networking, the NBCUSA, Inc., maintains an affiliation with the National and World Councils of Churches and the Congress of National Black Churches.

PROGRESSIVE NATIONAL BAPTIST
CONVENTION, INC.

The Progressive National Baptists came into existence in 1961 as an affirmation of a democratic, relevant, and progressive fellowship. It was organized in Zion Baptist Church, Cincinnati, Ohio, after circulating a call letter to the pastors of the National Baptist Convention of the U.S.A. A disagreement had arisen in the National Convention, after revision of its constitution in 1952, concerning the interpretation of limited or lifetime tenure for its national officers. Clearly opting for limited tenure, the Progressive National Baptist Convention, Inc., adopted the following preamble to its own constitution:

The people called Progressive Baptists believe in the principles, tenets, and doctrines proclaimed or advocated in the New Testament as sufficient for their polity and practices. In Church government Baptists believe in the rule of the people, by the people, and for the people, and in the vestment of the authority and power to act in the majority. Therefore, we, the members of the Progressive National Baptist Convention, U.S.A., Inc., federate ourselves together in the name of and under the direction and guidance of God, sharing our common faith in Jesus Christ and our concern for strengthening God's work through our

common activities, and establish this Constitution for the
Progressive National Baptist Convention, U.S.A., Inc.

Major Doctrines
There are no significant doctrinal differences between the
Progressives and other Baptist Conventions, or with the general
concept of Baptists that acknowledges the individual's responsibility and authority to discern religious truth in communion
with God and in fellowship with Jesus. The Progressives emphasize the importance of that individual discernment in the
life of local, state, and national church structures as well.

Geography
Having been organized in 1961 and incorporated in 1963
and headquartered in Washington, D.C., the Progressive Baptists have grown from a small fellowship of thirty-three members
from fourteen states to more than a million members in over a
thousand churches in thirty-five cities. Some clergy are members
of more than one Baptist Convention. There are four regions
that meet annually — Southern, Southwestern, Midwestern, and
Eastern.

Organization
A major distinguishing feature of the Progressives is in its
organizational structure. Any regular Baptist church, association, state, fellowship, or convention that subscribes to the
tenets of the Progressives is welcomed. Member bodies contribute one percent of their churches' annual receipts of their
operating budget to the Convention, and a delegation based
upon membership size of the local church represents that church
at the annual meeting of the Convention. Each of the four regions meets annually, and three of them have Congress of Christian Education sessions during their regional meetings, the Congress being the largest of the auxiliary units of the Convention.
There is a strong, well-organized Women's Auxiliary that supports missions, evangelism, education, citizenship, child welfare, civil rights, and related concerns. National meetings of
Progressive Laymen are held twice a year, and the men support

special projects as well as the Convention program. Church ushers and youth also hold their own meetings and support various programs.

In addition to the regions and auxiliary groups, there is an Executive Board that brings together the officers, staff, auxiliary heads, and state organization heads to act in an interim capacity for the Convention. The Progressive National Baptists have a Baptist Foreign Mission Bureau, Home Mission Board, and Board of Education as well as a Publishing Board, which produces Sunday School and other Christian education materials.

There is a general secretary to administer the operation of the Convention and the headquarters staff. All officers are elected and cannot succeed themselves after two years in the same position. The Convention has a unified budget. It supports a number of institutions, especially Black educational institutions such as Morehouse School of Religion, Virginia Union University, Shaw University, Bishop College, Morris College, and Howard University School of Religion.

Worship

As in other Black churches, worship is considered essential for the Progressives, who share a general Baptist history, to press the meaning and role of worship and Black church leadership into the future. Vincent Harding eloquently raises these possibilities:

Seeing ourselves and them in a new way, we will realize how deeply the Native American movements and the ecology forces are tied to the best insights of our own African forbears regarding the mutually nurturing relationships of human beings to the spirit-filled earth, waters, and skies. We will recognize how much unfinished business there is between Black men and Black women and how grateful we must all be for a women's movement whose most recent state and shape owe so much to our own struggle.

He further postulates that from the 1970s onward there may be a "fundamental turning point in the political, economic, ecolog-

ical, and spiritual relationships of the world, bearing the inti-
mations of a transformation that is destined to take us beyond
the civilization of the industrial revolution, preparing us for the
demands of the twenty-first century."

One of the powerful voices of the Progressive Baptist tradition is Martin Luther King, whose theology of hope draws from
and participates in the Black church worship experience. King
said at various occasions regarding hope:

> ...genuine hope involves a recognition. It involves a
> recognition that what is hoped for is already here. It is al-
> ready present, in the sense that it is a power which drives
> us to fulfill that which we hope for...hope is a final refusal
> to give up.... It means going on *anyhow*.
> ...realistic hope is based on a willingness to face the
> risk of failure and embrace an in-spite-of quality."
> ...hope has a "we" quality. And this is why hope is
> always contagious...hope is something of the tension be-
> tween present and future.
> ...When you lose hope you lose creativity, you lose ra-
> tionality. Hope is necessary for creativity and spirituality.
> Hope is one of the basic structures for an adequate life.

Ecumenical Involvement

The Progressive Baptists are participants in the Baptist World
Alliance, the North America Baptist Fellowship, the Baptist
Joint Committee on Public Affairs, and the National and World
Councils of Churches, the Washington Office on Africa, and
Interfaith Action for Economic Justice. They also support such
social programs as the Martin Luther King Center for Social
Change, the SCLC, Urban League, and the NAACP.

4

ORTHODOX CHURCHES

The churches in the United States that are related to the Orthodox tradition often have a particular cultural heritage — the Greek Orthodox Church, the Syrian Orthodox, the Armenian, the Antiochian, for example. Yet they have Orthodoxy in common.

Early Christianity struggled to maintain unity despite differences in theological understanding, language, culture and politics. Ecumenical Councils were means of mediating these differences that challenged the catholicity of the church — Nicaea in A.D. 325, Constantinople in 381, and Ephesus in 431. The Council of Chalcedon, the fourth Ecumenical Council (451), was convened by Emperor Marcian to unite the church, but a controversy over a formulation for the unity of Christ's divine and human nature became the theological thorn over which the Copts, Armenians, Ethiopians, and Syrians separated from the rest. They were participating to some degree also in the cultural divisions around the Mediterranean Sea and the political tensions that split the once-monolithic empire into east and west, Constantinople and Rome as the respective centers of the

Byzantine and Roman Empires. The churches that rejected the Council of Chalcedon are known as the Oriental Orthodox, or pre-Chalcedonian, family.

By 1054 the church had divided again between Rome and Byzantium, between Latin culture and Greek. The primary theological issue was the controversy over the "filioque" clause in the Nicene-Constantinopolitan Creed. Also at issue were the claims of the Roman pope. Cultural and political differences compounded these issues, and the Crusades brought the separate hierarchies into confrontation. Despite several early efforts to reunite them, Roman Catholics and the Eastern Orthodox remain distinct to the present day, although there has been recent progress in mediating theological differences.

The Eastern Orthodox churches (Antiochian, Greek, Orthodox Church in America, Russian, Serbian, and Ukrainian) are also separate from the Oriental Orthodox churches, by the decision of the Oriental churches to reject the Council of Chalcedon. In 1959 the Ecumenical Patriarch of Constantinople, while addressing the Copts, said, "In truth we are all one, we are all Orthodox Christians.... We have the same sacraments, the same history, the same traditions. The divergence is on the level of phraseology."

Orthodox scholar Kallistos Ware, expressing the yearning for unity that characterizes Orthodoxy, warns, "We know where the Church is but we cannot be sure where it is not; and so we must refrain from passing judgment on non-Orthodox Christians."

Before examining the unique histories of each of the Orthodox churches, an examination of common doctrine and worship for the Eastern Orthodox churches and also for the Oriental Orthodox churches is in order. These two groups need to be discussed separately, because the years of living as distinct communities of faith have introduced distinctive theology and practice as well.

EASTERN ORTHODOXY

Major Doctrines

The first seven Ecumenical Councils, prior to the one in 869–870 in Constantinople, which is considered the Eighth Ecumenical Council by the Roman Catholic Church, constitute the living tradition of Eastern Orthodoxy. Kallistos Ware stresses the importance of "living continuity," or tradition, among the Orthodox. Tradition includes the books of the Bible, the Nicene Creed, the decrees of the Ecumenical Councils, the writings of the Fathers, the Canons, the Service Books, the Holy Icons — indeed, the entire system of doctrine, government, worship, and art that Orthodoxy has articulated and preserved throughout the ages. Of these, the Bible, the Creed, and doctrinal definitions of the Ecumenical Councils are central. As heirs and guardians of the great inheritance, the Orthodox Christians of today preserve and pass along this tradition to the next generation. Doctrinal decisions of the Ecumenical Councils are understood as infallible once received by the church.

"Orthodoxy" means "right praise" or "right belief," and the faithful are called to "right action" (*orthopraxia*). Orthodoxy recognizes spiritual concerns as the most important aspects of human living; all of life is subject to the criterion of the Holy Spirit. Something of the spirit of Orthodox theology is captured in the chapter headings of Ware's *The Orthodox Way:* God as Mystery, as Trinity, as Creator, as Man (Human), as Spirit, as Prayer, and as Eternity. Theoretical theology in Orthodoxy is indivisibly linked with spiritual life.

Russian Orthodox Fr. Georges Florovsky says:

The Church gives us not a system, but a key; not a plan of God's City, but the means of entering it. Perhaps someone will lose his way because he has no plan. But all that he will see, he will see without a mediator, he will see it directly, it

will be real for him; while he who has studied only the plan
risks remaining outside and not really finding anything.

(Although this quotation and the dominant ethos of Orthodoxy
are masculine, women are a faithful mainstay of congregational
life.) Archbishop Paul of Finland echoes a similar thought:

> Not even in our day is the Christian faith a philosophy
> or an ideology; it is an encounter with Christ. The same
> three things — faith, *ecclesia* and *eucharistia* — still lead to
> this encounter. Together they are a framework instituted
> by God, through which the new life of Christ is given to
> the world.

The Orthodox concept of tradition is dynamic, for it lives
within the church as a living experience of the Holy Spirit.
Although tradition, because God does not change, is inwardly
changeless, it still seeks new formulations that add new understanding without negating past statements of faith. It is possible
that someday there will be a new Ecumenical Council that will
amplify and enrich the work of previous councils. As Georges
Florovsky describes it, "Tradition is the constant abiding of the
Spirit and not only the memory of words."

Worship
Orthodox worship is one of the great gifts this tradition
brings to the ecumenical movement. Each day begins, as in
Judaism, with sunset; there is within every twenty-four hours a
liturgical cycle, and there is a weekly system in which each day
plays a special role culminating in the Lord's Day of resurrection. There are a number of seasons for fasting, and a liturgical
year whose sacred signs become a source of grace. The celebration of the Eucharist constitutes the perpetual festival of the
church, a true feast, a participation in the joy of the resurrection
and the Kingdom that is to come. The coming to God in prayer
and solemn festival is understood in Orthodoxy to be the cease-
less coming of God in power and glory. A treasury of creativity
in the form of hymnody, icons, architecture, and sacred songs

has flourished through the centrality of worship in the Orthodox tradition.

"The Orthodox approach to religion is fundamentally a liturgical approach, which understands doctrine in the context of divine worship; it is no coincidence that the word 'Orthodoxy' should signify alike right belief and right worship, for the two things are inseparable," says Kallistos Ware. The sense of corporate worship is very important, and the liturgy belongs to the whole Christian people; it is not just the "preserve of the learned and the clergy." Immigrants settling in North America can feel "at home" in the Holy Liturgy, from which they draw inspiration, hope, and a sense of "heaven on earth," despite the strangeness of their new surroundings.

The true aim of the Christian life, say the Orthodox, is the acquisition of the Holy Spirit of God. Prayers, fastings, vigils, and other good works are means to that end. Much of the doctrine of Orthodoxy is expressed through liturgical worship, in which tradition is "handed down to us in a mystery." Not only the words of the service, but the gestures and actions have special symbolic meaning and often dramatize the truths of the faith.

The Eastern Orthodox Church, for example, celebrates the liturgies of St. John Chrysostom, St. Basil the Great, and of the Presanctified Gifts. As a history written under the direction of Patriarch Aleksy of Moscow describes the liturgy:

> Characteristic traits of the Russian Orthodox divine service are its unhurriedness, lengthiness. In an atmosphere which helps to relieve emotional tension, irritability, and the sense of haste, the consciousness learns to sink into sacred silence — *hesychia*, in which the Word of God resounds.

Veneration of the Virgin Mary as Queen of Heaven is one of the most characteristic manifestations of Eastern Orthodox piety, and she is requested to beseech her Son to forgive sins, save souls, and spare them eternal torment. Orthodox piety also venerates the saints, who are intercessors before God. Holy water blessed during the Epiphany is kept in every believer's home and used during illness and spiritual anxiety. The Orthodox devout pray in church and light candles in front of icons of the Savior, Mary and the saints.

The Eastern Orthodox stress icons as one of the ways whereby God is revealed to humanity. Icons reflect, through the skill of the artist and within certain prescribed rules, the mind of the church, giving the Orthodox Christian a vision of the spiritual world. The Bible is understood as the verbal icon of Christ. Another special gift of worship and spiritual enrichment is the *Philokalia*, an anthology of over a thousand pages of spiritual writings, concerned with the theory and practice of prayer, especially the "Jesus Prayer." This work was instrumental in producing a spiritual reawakening in nineteenth-century Russia, according to Kallistos Ware. The Jesus Prayer ("Lord Jesus Christ, Son of God, have mercy on me a sinner") is sometimes linked to certain physical exercises that assist concentration.

A living, personal, prayerful communion with God and a striving for spiritual perfection that draws a person closer to God are the goal of an Orthodox believer's spiritual life. A woman with child prepares the way for the child before birth by attending church and taking Holy Communion more frequently. In believers' families children are baptized in their infancy. Chrismation (anointing with holy oil) is performed at the time of Baptism for receiving the gifts of the Holy Spirit. Up until the age of seven children receive Holy Communion without confession, but after that they bear responsibility for their actions and participate in confession. Orthodox confession does not mean a simple listing of one's sins, but the obligatory examination of the correctness of one's inner life, repentance for errors, and firm resolution to change. Bible study and participation in the sacraments round out the spiritual life of the faithful. Matrimony is a sacrament that fuses two persons into one life and one flesh. During serious illness the Sacrament of Holy Unction is administered. While the people are acknowledged to be the keepers of piety, the priests are stewards of the mysteries of God and are responsible for the spiritual destiny of their flock.

THE ANTIOCHIAN ORTHODOX CHRISTIAN ARCHDIOCESE OF NORTH AMERICA

The year 1985 was a "Holy Antiochian Year," celebrated in part by the visit to the United States of His Beatitude Patriarch Ignatius IV of the Eastern Orthodox Patriarchate of Antioch and All the East, headquartered in Damascus, Syria. He said, "I see that all the life of our Archdiocese cannot forget its general context: it is ANTIOCHIAN, it is ORTHODOX, it is in NORTH AMERICA." By "Orthodox" he means the Chalcedonian supporters who did not separate from the Roman Catholics until around A.D. 1000.

The Archdiocese is in fact a joining of two former Archdioceses, one centered in New York and the other in Toledo, Ohio, recognized as one in 1975 by the Holy Synod of the Patriarchate of Antioch and All the East. Prior to this union there had been two missions to Syrian and Lebanese immigrants in the United States, one the Syrian mission of the Russian Orthodox Church and the other the Antiochian patriarchate; both of the missions united in 1936. An English-speaking group of converts to Orthodoxy was also incorporated into the Antiochian Church, and it was authorized to use the Western rites (purified of heterodox elements), to furnish their churches Western style (no iconostasis, for instance), and to wear Western liturgical vestments.

This complex description of the origins of the Antiochian Orthodox Christian Archdiocese of North America illustrates the interconnectedness of the Eastern Orthodox churches. St. Cyprian of Carthage (d. 258) saw all bishops as sharing in the one episcopate, yet sharing in a way that allows each to possess not a part but the whole: "So is the Church a single whole, though it spreads far and wide into a multitude of churches as its fertility increases." The Eastern Orthodox are a family of sister churches, decentralized in structure and with their own autonomy. Orthodox believe their church to be the true Church, and they yearn for the unity of all Christians within Orthodoxy.

In the U.S., however, the Eastern Orthodox churches are working to discover the shape of their own unity in a nation that gathers together many nationalities — and thus for the Orthodox, many "autonomies" of church structure. Perhaps this is best illustrated by a paragraph from a report by Father Paul Schneirla of the Department of Inter-Orthodox and Inter-Faith Relations, under the heading "The Reality":

> The American Church is now broadly constituted in four segments. Largest, best organized and richest, is the Greek Archdiocese with dependent Albanian, Carpatho-Russian, Ukrainian and Byelo-Russian jurisdictions. Next in size is the Orthodox Church in America (formerly the Russian Metropolia) with dependent Albanian, Bulgarian and Romanian jurisdictions. A third grouping, without direct canonical ties with each other, is made up of our Archdiocese and the canonical Serbians, Romanians and Bulgarians. Ours is the largest and best acclimated to the general American scene. A fourth element consists of the Serbian and Ukrainian bodies which have no ties to each other or any primary jurisdictions. The Orthodox community then shades off into shadow groups claiming, perhaps with some legitimacy, to be filiations of Alexandria or Bucharest....

The Antiochian Archdiocese is a member of the Standing Conference of Orthodox Bishops (SCOBA) and thus is represented in the theological consultation with Roman Catholics, Anglicans and Lutherans. These dialogues are supervised by the Ecumenical Commission of SCOBA, and there are counterparts to the American dialogues on the international level. The Archdiocese is engaged in a bilateral-lateral dialogue with the Orthodox Church of America. It is also in contact with two other groups, neither of which, says Fr. Schneirla, is "precisely Orthodox": the Polish National Catholic Church and the Evangelical Orthodox Church, which resulted from study by a Protestant fundamentalist fellowship of early Christian history and the Fathers "in a sort of spiritual spontaneous combustion and a self-organized 'Orthodox Church.'"

Geography

With a membership largely of Syrian and Lebanese immigrants in the U.S., the Antiochian Orthodox Archdiocese is under the jurisdiction of the Patriarchate of Antioch. The Patriarch, who has been of Arab descent since 1899, resides in Damascus and consecrates the archbishops of the North American Archdiocese. Currently, headquarters of the Archdiocese are located at 358 Mountain Road, Englewood, New Jersey. The 1985 General Convention of the Archdiocese Statistical Reports lists 127 parishes, 14 of them in Canada. Total communicants are about 35,000, although inclusive membership among Lebanese and Syrians is estimated as high as 280,000. The Eastern and Midwestern regions of the United States contain 75 of the 127 parishes and over 50 percent of total communicants. There are 169 clergy in the Archdiocese. Provision for western Christians whose remote ancestors were Orthodox and who worship in a western liturgical style is accomplished through a Western Rite within the Archdiocese.

Organization

The Patriarch is the head of an autocephalous (literally, self-headed) church. The Antiochian Archdiocese (joining two separate dioceses in 1975) has as its primate a metropolitan, who at the present time is the Most Reverend Metropolitan Philip Saliba. Next in the hierarchy is the archbishop. Priests may be married before becoming ordained. There are three "major orders": bishop, priest, and deacon, with two "minor orders": sub-deacon and reader. Bishops are drawn exclusively from the monastic clergy. This is standard for all Eastern Orthodox churches.

Ecumenical Involvement

The Antiochian Orthodox Archdiocese was the first Orthodox church to enter the Federal Council of Churches, predecessor of the National Council of Churches, and it is active in the National Council today. For a time the Archdiocese had separate representation in the World Council of Churches, but since 1983 it participates through the Patriarchate in Damascus. It also participates in several ecumenical dialogues and is a member of the Standing Conference of Orthodox Bishops.

THE GREEK ORTHODOX ARCHDIOCESE
OF NORTH AND SOUTH AMERICA

Just as other church traditions reach back to New Testament figures for their origins, so the Greeks remember the Apostle Paul's missionary journeys that established the Greek church. Out of these earliest beginnings there arose four great patriarchates that continue today: Constantinople, Alexandria, Antioch, and Jerusalem. During the Chalcedon controversy, described in more detail in profiles of Syrian, Coptic, and Armenian Orthodox churches, the churches of Semitic culture separated from the others, their center being the Patriarchate of Alexandria. By 1054 the church had divided again between Rome and Byzantium, between Latin culture and Greek.

For many centuries the church in Greece was identified inseparably with the Ecumenical Patriarchate of Constantinople. However, political forces from outside the church have repeatedly influenced the history of the Christian church. When the Turks overturned the Byzantine Empire, they ruled the Christians with both tolerance and condescension. The Orthodox church was shaped into a civil as well as a religious institution, a confusion that confronts Orthodoxy to this day. The patriarchate was a tax collector as well as being expected to supply law-abiding citizens loyal to the Turkish government. When the Greeks achieved liberation from the Turks through revolution in 1830, they also became an autocephalous church in 1833, breaking canonical relations with the Ecumenical Patriarchate. This history is important for understanding the turmoil of the Greek Orthodox Church as it found its way through immigrants to the United States, the first of whom arrived in New Orleans in 1864. Although many immigrants looked upon themselves as temporary citizens, eventually to return to Greece, others began the arduous task of establishing churches. Overwhelmed by the politics of Europe, the Ecumenical Patriarch of Constantinople placed the immigrant churches under the Church of Greece, which was similarly preoccupied. Also, canon law forbids the appointment of a bishop in a province where a canonical bishop already exists, and there were already bishops of the Church of Russia in the U.S. Transplanted Greeks, often shunned or urged to "Americanize," sought church relationships of their own nationality, even if that meant accepting leaders who lacked proper ecclesiastical lineage and training.

The first Greek Orthodox bishop, Meletios Metaxakis, arrived in the U.S. in 1918 to organize what had become a chaotic situation. Political conflict between royalists and supporters of Venizelos back in Greece only added further confusion, and Metaxakis was deposed, but not before he had called the first congress for incorporating into the Greek Orthodox Archdiocese of North and South America. By 1921 he had become the Ecumenical Patriarch of Constantinople. Subsequently, there were fierce struggles over leadership, and historian Peter Kourides described the period of Archbishop Alexander's reign as "an undisciplined nightmare," in which the politics of the world and the politics of the church outdid one another to damage the church.

The three archbishops that followed — Athenagoras, Michael, and now Iakovos — have achieved remarkable stability, discipline and vision for the Greek Church. Persuasively reconciling, Athenagoras "towered gauntly over men like an El Greco saint, with luminous, searching and penetrating eyes," describes Kourides. He established the Holy Cross Theological Seminary and a home for orphans called St. Basil Academy, and recognized the indispensable work of the women by legally chartering the national Philoptochos organization in 1944. When he left to become the Ecumenical Patriarch, he departed on President Truman's private plane ("The Sacred Cow"). Having come to the U.S. without one newspaper word of welcome in 1931, he left with his photograph on the cover of *Life* magazine.

Similarly, Michael consolidated and extended the unity and reconciliation that Athenagoras had begun, managing to increase the revenue of the Archdiocese sixfold and organizing GOYA, the Greek Orthodox Youth of America. When the Cathedral of St. Sophia in Washington was dedicated in 1956, the U.S. president, vice president, and secretary of state participated. For an immigrant church, this was an important symbol.

Since 1958 Archbishop Iakovos has served the Archdiocese, strengthening its ties with the Patriarchate of Constantinople and bringing his Harvard theological training to bear upon the demands of a maturing church. One of his goals has been to overcome the self-induced inferiority limitations of an immigrant self-image, in part by cultivating the media and involving the church ecumenically at national and world levels.

Geography

The Patriarchate of Constantinople includes Turkey, Crete and other Aegean islands, Mount Athos (with twenty monasteries), Finland, and all Greeks of the dispersion, as well as some Russian, Ukrainian, Polish, and Albanian dioceses in emigration. In total this amounts to about three million persons, about half of whom are in North America. The Archdiocese has districts in Canada, South America, Central America, and eight in the United States.

Organization

In addition to the districts mentioned above, the Greek Orthodox Archbishop of North and South America serves as hemispheric exarch of the ecumenical patriarch, exercising spiritual supervision over the American Carpatho-Russian Orthodox Greek Catholic Diocese and the Ukrainian Orthodox Church of America. These jurisdictions function in total independence, however, and their bishops are members of the Standing Con-

ference of Canonical Orthodox Bishops in the Americas, as are
the Greek Orthodox.

Ecumenical Involvement

Under Archbishop Michael the Archdiocese joined the National Council of Churches and the World Council of Churches.
Archbishop Iakovos was at one time the representative of the ecumenical patriarch to the World Council of Churches in Geneva,
later serving as a WCC president. The Archdiocese participates
in SCOBA (Standing Conference of Canonical Orthodox Bishops in the Americas). The women of the Philoptochos organization are active in Church Women United.

THE ORTHODOX CHURCH IN AMERICA

A mission in Alaska, established in 1794 by monks of the Russian Orthodox Church, begins the story of the Orthodox Church in America. Following the sale of Alaska to the United States by the Russian Empire in 1867, the mission became in 1870 the Diocese of the Aleutian Islands and Alaska. In 1872 the See was moved from Sitka to San Francisco, and in 1900 its name was changed to Diocese of the Aleutian Islands and North America.

Archbishop Tikhon moved the See to New York City in 1905, where a temple (St. Nicholas) worthy of becoming a cathedral had already been erected through the foresight and fundraising of Father Alexander Hotovitsky. Tikhon had a vision, enunciated publicly in 1906, the year before his new assignment to the See of Yaroslav, that the Orthodox Church of America, which already encompassed parishes of many different nationalities, would be granted an unusual autonomy because of the peculiarities of American life. The bishops of the various ethnic groups would come together as a General Council, presided over by the Russian Archbishop, through whom would be preserved the connection of the Orthodox Church of America with its founder, the Church of Russia.

As a first step, the First All-American Sobor (or Council), which was comprised of representatives of the laity, clergy and bishops of the American Church, voted in 1907 to become "The

135

Russian Orthodox Greek-Catholic Church in North America under the Hierarchy of the Russian Church," in order to make the Uniates who had moved to the United States more comfortable about returning to their Orthodox heritage. (The Uniates, under the Union of Brest-Litovsk in 1596, had recognized the supremacy of the pope while retaining their own Orthodox ecclesiastical practices and liturgy.) During the seven-year administration of Archbishop Platon (1907–1914), the Diocese received no less than 72 such parishes, most of which were of Carpatho-Russian background.

But the anarchy that afflicted the Russian Orthodox Church during and immediately following the Communist revolution in 1917 spilled over into the United States, destroying any immediate hope for a fully united Orthodox Church in America as Tikhon, who would become Patriarch of Moscow in 1917, had envisioned. Political immigrants, including clergy, began to arrive from the new Soviet Union; authority was undermined; and the demand in 1931 by the Moscow Patriarchate for political submission to the USSR as a condition for restoration of church relations was unacceptable. This demand of the Moscow Patriarchate had been resisted by Patriarch Tikhon until his death; his successor, Sergius, under severe pressure from the civil authorities, complied.

In 1970 the Russian Orthodox Church granted complete self-government, or "autocephaly," to the Russian Orthodox Greek Catholic Church in North America and expressed the intention for it to be the instrument of unity for all Orthodox in America, through its new name, the Orthodox Church in America. It is the only self-governing Orthodox Church in the new world outside of traditional Orthodox lands. Today, 90 percent of its parishes use the English language in their services. Its parishes are constituted primarily of third- and fourth-generation Americans in addition to a large percentage of converts.

Geography

The jurisdiction of the Orthodox Church in America extends over North and South America, including the United States, Canada, and, since 1972, Mexico. There are twelve dioceses in the United States and one each in Canada, Mexico, and South America, with an inclusive membership of about a million. Among the dioceses are the Romanian, Albanian, and Bulgarian dioceses, which joined the OCA in 1960, 1971, and 1976, respectively. They are within the canonical jurisdiction of the OCA, but enjoy a certain amount of administrative autonomy. In addition, a missionary diocese in the southern United States is thriving, as is the Diocese of Alaska, which continues to minister to the spiritual needs of Native Americans, as it has for nearly 200 years.

Aware of a recent survey showing that 46 percent of the parishes have grown in membership and 40 percent had declined, the OCA emphasized evangelization at its Eighth All-American Council in the fall of 1986. Youth programs are a major effort of the OCA, and its young people participate in Syndesmos, an international Orthodox youth movement founded in 1953.

Organization

The All-American Council, the highest legislative and administrative authority within the church, reviews the programs, finances, and priorities of the church. Unusual in world Orthodoxy, bishops, priests and lay delegates make decisions together in the All-American Council in the OCA. These decisions must be finally approved after examination by the Holy Synod of Bishops. The Holy Synod meets twice a year. There is also a lesser Synod, which is authorized by the Holy Synod to make provisional decisions about certain matters. Presiding over both is the primate of the church, currently Metropolitan Theodosius.

Ecumenical Involvement

The Orthodox Church in America participates in the National and World Councils of Churches and in the Standing Conference of Canonical Orthodox Bishops in the Americas.

PATRIARCHAL PARISHES
OF THE RUSSIAN ORTHODOX CHURCH
IN THE UNITED STATES AND CANADA

"In the years between the two World Wars the Christians of Russia underwent sufferings which in extent and in cruelty equalled anything endured by the early Christians," states Kallistos Ware. Behind this chilling statement stand the ranks of imprisonments, killings, confiscations of property, intimidations, desecrations, and other persecutions of the church whose exact dimensions and numbers are known only to God. In large measure this reality explains the present fracturing in the United States of Orthodox churches with Russian origins.

The Patriarchal Parishes have a common history with the Orthodox Church in America, formerly the Metropolia of the Russian Orthodox Church, as far back as 1794, the date of the founding of the mission in Alaska. After the Revolution of 1917, however, the newly elected Patriarch Tikhon, despite his personal qualities of leadership, was unable under civil war conditions to administer dioceses separated by civil strife.

In 1920, acting on the basis of a directive issued by Patriarch Tikhon and still under some dispute, the bishops of the Russian Orthodox Church who found themselves in precisely such a situation of administrative separation established the Supreme Church Administration for Churches Outside of Russia. At first it maintained its canonical ties to Patriarch Tikhon, while at the same time establishing semi-autonomous Metropolitan Districts for local diocesan administration in Europe, the Balkans, China, and North America. Having its headquarters first in Istanbul, then in Yugoslavia, the Russian Orthodox Church Outside Russia eventually moved its headquarters to Munich, Germany, and in 1950 to New York City. With the death of Patriarch Tikhon in 1925 and the beginning of the administration of the Deputy Locum Tenens of the Patriarchal Throne, Metropolitan Sergii (Sergius), in 1927, it severed canonical ties to the Russian Orthodox Church, because of its belief that the Communist government in Russia completely controls the Patriarchate.

In 1924, the Metropolitan District of North America (or "Metropolia," which became the Orthodox Church in America in 1970) declared complete autonomy from both the Patriarchate and from the Russian Orthodox Church Outside Russia. Metropolitan Sergii and the Sacred Synod of the Russian Orthodox Church reestablished in 1933 their ecclesiastical control over those parishes of the North American Diocese that had remained faithful to Mother Church, establishing the Archdiocese of New York and the Aleutian Islands as an Exarchate of the Patriarch of Moscow. Metropolitan Benjamin Fedchenkov from France was assigned to the post of Patriarchal Exarch.

From 1936 to 1946 the "Metropolia" (OCA) was aligned with the Russian Orthodox Church Outside of Russia. In 1946 recognition of the autonomy of the American church was sought from the Russian church. Upon petition to the Russian Orthodox Church in 1970, it was granted autocephalous status and recognized by its new name, the Orthodox Church in America. At the same time, the Russian Orthodox Church dissolved its own Exarchate — the Archdiocese of New York and the Aleutian Islands. Those parishes that chose to remain within the structure of the Russian Orthodox Church were reorganized to form a new entity, the Patriarchal Parishes of the Russian Orthodox Church, administered directly by the Patriarch of Moscow through one of his vicar bishops. This structure will continue until such time as these parishes freely choose to enter the jurisdiction of the autocephalous Orthodox Church in America.

Geography

The Patriarchal Parishes in the United States number about forty-one churches, with an inclusive membership of 51,500, and in Canada there are roughly 8,000 members and twenty-four churches. Headquarters are in New York City.

Organization

A vicar bishop for the parishes serves under the Patriarch of Moscow. Having pledged to cooperate with the Orthodox Church in America even as they voted in 1970 to stay with the Mother Church, the Church of Russia, the Patriarchal Parishes support the OCA by prayer and action, and several priests and parishes have transferred in recent years to the OCA.

Ecumenical Involvement

The Patriarchal Parishes belong to the National Council of Churches. Through the Russian Orthodox Church they participate in the World Council of Churches and in continuing ecumenical conversations and dialogues, Pan Orthodox Conferences, and Inter-Orthodox Theological Commissions.

SERBIAN ORTHODOX CHURCH
IN THE U.S.A. AND CANADA

Like the other Eastern Orthodox churches, the Serbians trace their origins back to the early church, the Serbian Orthodox Church having acquired autocephaly from the Ecumenical Patriarchate of Nicaea in 1219 and recognition as a patriarchate by Constantinople in 1375. They also experience the disruptions of transplantation to a new continent.

Serbian immigrants to the United States from Eastern Europe had begun to arrive by the time of the American Civil War, although the first parish church was established only in 1894 in Jackson, California, with the blessing of the Russian Bishop. Named St. Sava's, it was the result of the labors of Fr. Sebastian Dabovitch, who was born in San Francisco of Serbian parents. Fr. Sebastian studied in Petrograd (now Leningrad, Russia) and returned to the U.S. to be ordained by Bishop Nicholas and to serve the Russian Cathedral in San Francisco until he was appointed pastor of St. Sava's Church.

Soon there were enough parishes to form the North American Diocese of the Russian Church. In 1913 a dozen parishes held a convention and requested release from the Russian diocese to come under the authority of the autocephalous Church of Serbia. World War I delayed immediate action, but, after investigation, the Holy Bishops' Council of the Serbian Orthodox

Church in Belgrade, Yugoslavia, accepted jurisdiction and appointed Archimandrite Mardarije as administrator of the new American diocese. Thus in 1923 at another Conference of Serbian Clergy, the American Serbian Orthodox diocese, by decision of the Church of Serbia, became self-governing and independent of the Russian Church.

After World War II, however, the Serbian Orthodox Church in Yugoslavia had to live in a complex new political environment. Rather than elevate the American diocese to a metropolitanate because of its continued growth, the Holy Council of Bishops created three dioceses out of one. Bishop Dionisije, who succeeded Mardarije, opposed this decision and was also embroiled in misconduct charges; he refused to acknowledge his suspension and drew a number of sympathetic followers with him, forming the Serbian Orthodox Diocese in the United States of America and Canada. In 1963 this diocese met in a national assembly and proclaimed itself completely autonomous under Bishop Dionisije as long as "Yugoslavia is in the Communist slavery."

Civil courts supported Bishop Dionisije, but the United States Supreme Court, in 1976, reversed the Illinois Supreme Court by judging that the decisions of hierarchical religious tribunals should be taken as binding by civil courts. Bishop Dionisije and his followers had meanwhile come into communion with the "Ukrainian Orthodox Church of the United States of America" and the "Autocephalous Greek Orthodox Church of America," both bodies not in communion with world Orthodoxy. In 1975 the Serbian Orthodox Diocese placed itself under the jurisdiction of the Patriarchate of Alexandria, and the assistant to Bishop Dionisije, Bishop Ireney, was recognized by the patriarch as a canonical hierarch. Several other Orthodox bodies, including the head of SCOBA (Standing Conference of Orthodox Bishops in the Americas), have sided with the Serbian Orthodox Holy Synod in Yugoslavia in its suspension of Bishop Dionisije. The dioceses in the United States formed by the Serbian Orthodox Holy Synod now compose the Serbian Orthodox Church in the United States of America and Canada.

Geography

There are the Middle Eastern Diocese with the See in Detroit, the Middle Western Diocese with the See at the Monastery in Libertyville, Illinois, and the Western Diocese, whose See is in Los Angeles. Another diocese has been organized in Canada. Churches in these four dioceses have over a hundred thousand members.

Organization

The Serbian Orthodox Church in the United States of America and Canada maintains hierarchical and spiritual ties with the Serbian Orthodox Patriarch and Holy Synod in Yugoslavia.

Ecumenical Involvement

The Serbian Orthodox Church in the United States of America and Canada is a member of the National Council of Churches and its Holy Synod participates in the World Council of Churches. It participates in SCOBA, which is a voluntary association established to serve as an agency to centralize and coordinate the mission of the church, to act as a clearing house for common concerns, and to avoid overlapping or duplication of services and agencies. SCOBA has special departments for campus work, Christian education, military and other chaplaincies, regional clergy fellowships, and ecumenical relations.

THE UKRAINIAN ORTHODOX CHURCH
IN AMERICA

To begin to understand the Ukrainian Orthodox Church in America, one must first know the geography from which this immigrant church has come. The Ukraine, now one of the Soviet Socialist Republics, is bordered by Hungary, Czechoslovakia, Poland, Romania, the Black Sea, and the other Soviet Republics of Byelorussia, Moldavia, and the Russian Federal Republic.

Tradition says that St. Andrew first brought the Gospel to Kiev, the capital of the Ukraine. In the fifteenth century part of the Ukrainian national church came under the Moscow patriarchate. By the late seventeenth century all of the Ukraine was in the Church of Russia. During the Russian revolution of 1917, the Ukrainians sought independence, as did the Ukrainian Church from the Russian Orthodox Church. The Ukrainian Church declared itself autocephalous and named its own hierarchy. During the purges that followed under communism, over 2,000 priests, thirty-four bishops, and many of their lay people were killed.

Meanwhile, in the U.S. the Ukrainian Orthodox Church was being organized in 1919. Some of the immigrants were called "Ruthenians"; they had been peasant pawns during the attempt to unite Roman Catholics and Orthodox under the pope (the Union of Brest, 1596) and had become Uniates or Ruthenian Rite Roman Catholics. Once they had come to the United States and were no longer subject to the persecutions of Roman Catholic Polish gentry, they chose to return to Eastern Orthodoxy.

But determining, in its new American setting, the authentic episcopal authority of the Ukrainian Church out of the chaos of this briefly sketched European history has been extremely difficult. Metropolitan John Theodorovich, who had been consecrated by newly-independent bishops martyred during the communist revolution in the Ukraine, was unacceptable to Eastern Orthodox prelates in the U.S., including members of SCOBA (Standing Conference of Canonical Orthodox Bishops of the Americas). Theodorovich was not deterred, and one continuing group, not a member of the National Council of Churches, exists, despite its non-canonical status, as the Ukrainian Orthodox Church in the United States of America.

Through the efforts of SCOBA, Joseph A. Zuk, a former Ruthenian Rite Roman Catholic priest who had converted to Eastern Orthodoxy, was consecrated in 1932 as bishop of the Ukrainian Orthodox Church of America (Ecumenical Patriarchate). Under the next leader, Bishop Bohdan, who was consecrated by decision of the Ecumenical Patriarch of Constantinople in 1937, many small churches were brought under his supervision and a number of energetic young clergy were enlisted, some in a "tent-making ministry" capacity. At his death there was another challenge to leadership authority, and the church suffered severe attrition, but from 1966 Bishop Andrei Kuschak labored to rebuild this Ukrainian Orthodox body. There are several other Ukrainian Orthodox Churches, which also suffer the confusions of leadership that occur when secular political upheavals confound the ordinary stresses of succession to authority.

Geography

Headquarters of the Ukrainian Orthodox Church of America are located in Jamaica, New York. It numbers roughly 30,000, with thirty local congregations. The U.O.C.A. has attempted to find a moderate way between a Ukrainian nationalism that strictly requires the use of the Ukrainian language in its Divine Service and an accommodation to American culture. All immigrant churches face the dilemma of expressing pride in their own ethnic culture and openness to the new. The choice of language used in liturgy becomes a significant weight on one side or the other of these sometimes conflicting goals. Generational differences exacerbate the complexity of such choices.

Organization

The Ukrainian Orthodox Church of America receives its canonical authority from the Ecumenical Patriarchate of Constantinople. Ideally every priest receives an appropriate theological education, all bishops are duly consecrated, and the line of authority is clear and unbroken back to the ancient patriarchates. The nature of human society, shown in this brief history, sometimes tragically wreaks havoc with that ideal.

Ecumenical Involvement

The Ukrainian Orthodox Church of America is an active member of SCOBA and is also a member of the National Council of Churches of Christ in the U.S.A.

ORIENTAL ORTHODOXY

The Armenian, Coptic and Syrian Orthodox churches all subscribe to the pre-Chalcedonian creeds. That is, the first three Ecumenical Councils (Nicaea, Constantinople and Ephesus) form the basis of their doctrine. The profile of each of these three churches delineates further the nuances of their theologies and expression of faith in worship. Among the Oriental Orthodox, worship is also highly liturgical, each using a different language within its own cultural context.

147

THE ARMENIAN ORTHODOX CHURCH, DIOCESE OF THE ARMENIAN CHURCH OF AMERICA

Armenia was the first nation to adopt Christianity as its national faith (A.D. 301). Tradition says Thaddeus and Bartholomew, two of the twelve disciples, brought Christianity to the Armenians before they had an Armenian alphabet to record their history. An Armenian-born convert, St. Gregory the Illuminator, of a noble family, suffered much persecution before he succeeded in converting King Tiridates of Armenia to the faith. Gregory built with the king's help a cathedral near Mt. Ararat, now called Holy Etchmiadzin and still the official seat of the supreme head of the Armenian Orthodox Church. His son represented him at the First Ecumenical Council at Nicaea in 325.

Armenians were locked in deadly battle with the militarily superior Persians, defending their faith against Zoroastrianism, and could not participate in the Council at Chalcedon in 451. Although St. Vartan Mamigonian lost the battle, the war dragged on until Persia ceased to push its religious conquest. St. Vartan is commemorated today through the St. Vartan Cathedral in New York City and the recent celebration by Mayor Koch of Vartanants Day (February 6), in honor of one of the earliest struggles for freedom of worship and conscience in the world.

In 506 at Dvin, the seat of the Armenian catholicos, the Armenians proclaimed their belief in the formulations of the third of the Ecumenical Councils at Ephesus but rejected Nestorianism and the acts of the Council of Chalcedon, thus joining the Copts, Ethiopians, and Syrian Orthodox as non-Chalcedonian Orthodox churches. Through the centuries there have been serious efforts to reunite the Armenians with both the Greek and Latin churches, with both the Byzantine and Roman Empires. Except for a few who became the Armenian rite of the Catholic Church, the majority of Armenians never reunited, as church unity was continually overwhelmed by waves of political change. Muslim Arabs, Turks, Greeks, the Mamelukes — all battled over Armenian land, and the battered church moved the seat of its catholicoi from place to place, establishing ministries for its fleeing migrations of the faithful.

Under the Ottoman Empire the Armenian Patriarchate of Turkey was created in 1461, but only in 1863 did Armenian lay leaders succeed in drawing up a statute for administration of the Patriarchate reluctantly acceptable to the government. By 1920 the Turkish secular government annulled the statute, culminating a bloody massacre of hundreds of thousands of Armenians by the Turks between 1895 and 1920. The heaviest annihilation of the Armenian population took place in 1915 and during World War I, in which estimates of losses as high as 1,500,000 have been made. Of 5,000 clergy in 1915, only 400 survived by 1923. Over 100,000 Armenian women were kidnaped for Turkish harems. Besides the incalculable loss of human life there was a systematic effort to destroy Armenian culture, especially that of the churches. During World War I alone the Turks destroyed more than 2,500 monasteries and churches, many of them ancient, holy and architectural rarities. Artistic treasures, scholarly and literary writings, church vessels and vestments, artifacts in gold and silver, and extensive lands were pillaged, ransacked, sold, or destroyed. An entire people and culture have been nearly demolished in an attempted genocide. Persons either deported or fleeing the onslaught of terror settled elsewhere in the Middle East or as far away as North America. New monasteries and seminaries have had to be established to revitalize the exhausted church.

Once liberated from Persian rule by the Russians in 1828, the Armenian Republic is now within the Soviet Union, and a regulation (Polozhenie) under the czar for an agreement with the administration of the catholicate of Holy Etchmiadzin in 1836 has been abrogated by the Soviets. The hierarchical center of the Armenian Church is still Holy Etchmiadzin under the Supreme Patriarch Catholicos, the 130th pontiff since St. Gregory the Illuminator.

The Armenian genocide (still referred to as "alleged" by the U.S. State Department) is generally considered the first attempt to destroy an entire ethnic group in the twentieth century — by massacre, starvation, thirst, exposure, detention and exile. Interfaith materials have been prepared for use in memorial commemorations including the Orthodox prayer "... we pray for their executioners, asking You (God) to forgive them, for they certainly 'did not know what they were doing.' We pray for their successors in political power, to realize the mistake of their predecessors, and try to partially at least correct this mistake by genuinely expressing their sorrow for it."

Major Doctrines

Sharing the faith formulated in the first three Ecumenical Councils with the other Oriental Orthodox churches, the Armenians accept the Incarnation as expressed by St. Cyril of Alexandria. Christ is "without mother from the Father and without father from the Mother." They believe in original sin as inherited from Adam, salvation as a free gift of God, achieved by Christ's sacrifice of himself for sinners. Scripture is divinely inspired. Saints are revered and prayed to. Artistic representations of Christ and of the saints are venerated but not worshipped.

Geography

As the terror in Turkey began to take shape, many Armenians immigrated to North America in the 1880s, and the first Armenian parish was organized in Worcester, Massachusetts, in 1889. Catholicos Khrimian, founder of the Diocese of the Armenian Church of America in 1898, tried to call the attention of European diplomats to the plight of the Armenians under the

Turks, bravely defending his people before Ottoman officials and enduring exile for three years. He persuaded the czarist regime not to seize the treasury of Holy Etchmiadzin. There are now two dioceses in the U.S., the Eastern Diocese headquartered in New York, the Western in California, and a third is located in Canada (1984). A South American diocese was established in 1938 by the Catholicos of Etchmiadzin. There are roughly 500,000 communicants in North America, with about 25,000 dues-paying adult members. There are seventy-five clergy. In addition, there is another body of Armenians not counted in these numbers, who in a schism over political issues that divided the Armenian community in the U.S. placed themselves under the Catholicos of Cilicia (1956), and are called the Prelacy of the Armenian Apostolic Church of America. Unity Committees from both parts of the Armenian Church of America have been meeting for sixteen years, but with minimal progress. The Prelacy has a total membership of 225,000.

Organization

Laity possess much power in the Armenian Church, parishioners electing their parish priests by direct vote, and at least two-thirds of the electoral colleges that elect primates, patriarchs, and catholicoi are lay. Clergy may be married prior to ordination, but bishops are chosen from celibate clergy. The Catholicate of Etchmiadzin, seat of the Supreme Patriarch Catholicos, is the hierarchical center of the church, although the catholicos at Antelias, Lebanon, is Catholicos of the Great House of Cilicia, and there is some history of tension between them. The Prelacy of the Armenian Apostolic Church of America relates directly to Cilicia, but recognizes the primacy of honor of Etchmiadzin. One of four seminaries, St. Nersess, is located in the U.S. in New Rochelle, New York, administered by both Eastern and Western U.S. dioceses.

Worship

Baptism, confirmation and Holy Communion are administered together. Other sacraments include penance (preparation for Communion), ordination to holy orders, and marriage (sacrament of the "crowning"). Anointing of the sick is rarely administered and its status is not clear. Minor orders are the offices of doorkeepers, readers, exorcists, acolytes, and subdeacons. Major orders are the diaconate, priesthood and the episcopate. The Eucharist is understood as a mystery of transformation of the elements, in which the Eucharistic sacrifice is the same as the sacrifice of the cross in essence and power, but different in form. Use of icons is not encouraged, and instead of the iconostasis screen in front of the altar, Armenian churches have a curtain. The Divine Liturgy is chanted in classical Armenian, with priest, deacon and choir participating. Communion is by intinction, the wafer being circular, stamped with a cross, and baked by the priest on the day of the liturgy. The wine is undiluted.

Worship has sustained these Armenian people through centuries of harassment, oppression, and near-destruction. The Armenian language liturgy, religious music like that of the famed Gomidas, and instruction for recovering memory and awareness of Armenian culture such as the programs at St. Vartan's Cathedral in New York City are important restoratives to the Armenian soul.

Ecumenical Involvement

The Diocese of the Armenian Church of America is a member of the World Council of Churches (1963) and the National Council of Churches of Christ in the U.S.A. (1957). The Armenian Orthodox Church is in communion with the pre-Chalcedonian churches, known as the Oriental Orthodox churches.

THE COPTIC ORTHODOX CHURCH IN NORTH AMERICA

Christianity is believed to have come to Egypt as early as A.D. 48–55 through St. Mark, who is regarded as the first of 117 Patriarchs of Alexandria, as well as a saint and martyr (A.D. 68). Coptic Orthodox Christianity arrived in North America officially very recently — in 1965 the first parish was organized in Toronto, Canada, while in 1962 the Coptic Association of America was organized by Coptic immigrants in New York City, and Fr. Gabriel Abdelsayed established the first U.S. parish in 1970 in New York and New Jersey.

Alexandria's theological tradition from its earliest days is illustrious. Such notable Egyptian theologians as Pantaenus, Clement of Alexandria, Origen, Athanasius, and Cyril helped shape Christian thought. From the Catechetical School of Alexandria came great theological instruction, despite various Roman persecutions, especially during the reign of Diocletian, whose persecutions made the Copts date their Calendar of Martyrs from his accession in A.D. 284. Egypt was almost totally Christian by the fifth century, Christianity having been declared a state religion in 381, following the edict of Constantine the Great.

Rome, Constantinople, and Alexandria were the chief centers of church leadership as well as being rival political nodes of power. By the time of the fourth Ecumenical Council (after Nicaea in 325, Constantinople in 381, and Ephesus in 431) a combination of church rivalries, secular political machinations, and serious theological divisions made the work for unity at Chalcedon extremely precarious. At issue theologically was the formulation of the unity of Christ's divine and human nature while maintaining a clear and unconfusable distinction between them — "the Word made flesh." Intertwined with the subtleties of theological doctrine were loyalties to key theological figures and their geographical bases — such as Dioscurus and Cyril of Alexandria and Nestorius of Constantinople, all of whom were defeated by the acceptance of Roman Pope Leo's Tome, or Letter. Not only was Leo's formulation of the unity of Christ (perfect in Godhead, perfect in manhood...) adopted, but the Council of Chalcedon named Constantinople second only to Rome, shifting some of the leadership away from the Alexandrian See.

After the Chalcedonian controversy, whose council had been convened by Emperor Marcian to unite the church, the Coptic church rejected the Council of Chalcedon, despite several centuries of subsequent attempts to reunite them under Byzantine or Roman hegemony. The church was participating to some degree in the cultural divisions around the Mediterranean Sea and the political tensions that split the once-monolithic empire into east and west, with Constantinople and Rome as the respective centers of the Byzantine and Roman Empires. In the seventh century the Muslims conquered Egypt, ushering in an extended era of martyrdom, persecution and flight for many Copts. The Turkish conquest of Egypt in 1517 imposed further restrictions and destruction to Christian churches, a domination ending in 1798.

One serious attempt to unite the Coptic church to the Roman See in 1442 resulted in one segment accepting Roman Catholic authority and becoming a small Coptic rite. In more recent times there have been periods of relative religious freedom in Egypt, such as during the French and British occupation, and during the past thirty years the Copts have undergone a renaissance and a significant revival of Coptic theological learning.

Major Doctrines

Upholding St. Cyril's doctrine of the two natures of Christ — divine and human — mystically united in one, without confusion, corruption or change, the Copts are members of the Oriental Orthodox family (pre-Chalcedonian), subscribing to the early Ecumenical Councils and creeds up to Chalcedon. The other Oriental Orthodox, with whom they are in communion, are the Syrian Orthodox, Armenian Orthodox and Indian Orthodox. A major contribution of Egyptian Orthodoxy is monasticism, which began under the leadership of St. Anthony (c. 351–356) and whose monastic tradition came to flower in the Desert Fathers and was spread by such writings as St. Athanasius' *Life of the Saint*. St. Pachomius introduced cenobitism (solitary ascetic monks separate from a communal order) around A.D. 290.

Geography

Since the beginning of this century the number of Copts in Egypt has more than doubled in a country where Islam predominates. Copts exist outside of Egypt in Ethiopia, Europe, Asia, Australia, Canada, and the U.S., a world community estimated at 8 million, the vast majority being in Egypt. There are roughly 150,000 communicants in the U.S. and 50,000 in Canada, with dues-paying members of about 25,000. Currently there are twenty-five ordained priests in the U.S. and six in Canada. In the U.S. the Copts are mainly concentrated in the metropolitan areas of New York–New Jersey, Washington, D.C., Los Angeles, San Francisco, Chicago, Cleveland, Houston, Philadelphia, and Troy (Michigan). Canadian Copts are largely in Toronto and Montreal. Cairo, Egypt, is the hierarchical center of the See of St. Mark, where the central seminary is also located.

Organization

The Diocese of North America was established in 1965, with His Holiness the Pope as its immediate bishop. Diocesan headquarters are St. Mark in Toronto for Canada and St. Mark in New Jersey for the U.S. The present pope, Shenouda III, is "Pope of Alexandria and Patriarch of the See of St. Mark." He is the 117th successor of St. Mark and presides over all clergy and faithful. The "Pope" or "Papas" was a common title for bishops in the third to fifth centuries, and it was selected by the presbyters as the title for distinguishing the head of the bishops. Monks are required to be celibate, but priests may be married before they have been accepted for ordination. Monks alone are eligible for promotion to all ranks of the priesthood up to patriarch.

Worship

In Egypt the Divine Liturgy is celebrated in both Coptic and Arabic, though both Coptic and the language of everyday life are used in Coptic churches in other countries. Priests, deacons and the people all have their own particular part in the service. The Copts recognize seven sacraments. Baptism (by immersion), confirmation, and Holy Communion are administered to infants, immediately after birth if necessary. Usually they are administered together forty days after birth to boys and eighty days for girls. This allows the mother the canonical time required for cleansing, so that she will be ready for Holy Communion on the same day as her infant's Baptism. The other four sacraments are: penance (required before Holy Communion), anointing of the sick, matrimony and holy orders. In the Holy Eucharist the Holy Bread (Korban), a rounded loaf bearing the sign of the cross, is leavened and prepared on the same day of the Divine Liturgy. The wine must be fresh and undiluted. The Copts follow the St. Mark liturgy. Their calendar, which begins in September, has five fasts, including the 55-day Great Fast of Lent and the 42-day Fast of the Nativity preceding Christmas, which is celebrated according to the Julian calendar.

Ecumenical Involvement

The Copts are members of the World Council of Churches and the National Council of Churches, U.S.A.

THE SYRIAN ORTHODOX CHURCH
OF ANTIOCH, ARCHDIOCESE
OF NORTH AMERICA

Acts 11:26 confirms that the disciples were first called Christians in Antioch, thus laying the basis for the claim that the Patriarchate of Antioch is the oldest among the Christian churches. According to tradition, St. Peter established the See of Antioch, whose jurisdiction was all the territory between the Mediterranean Sea and the Persian Gulf, with missionary outreach as far as India and China.

The Syrian Orthodox Church of Antioch participated in and accepted the Ecumenical Councils of Nicaea (A.D. 325), Constantinople (381), and Ephesus (431), but, like the Copts, Armenians, and Ethiopians, rejected the decisions of the Council of Chalcedon (451). To the modern ear the terminologies of the Chalcedonians and the non-Chalcedonians do not seem far apart as they struggle to describe the mystery of Christ's divine yet human nature, united in the Incarnation uniquely, beyond the telling of it.

But there were very real cultural and political divisions involved, and severe persecutions occurred as the result of this rejection. In 518 Patriarch Severus was forced into exile in Egypt as the controversy between "Diaphorites" (literally "distinguishers," as dubbed by the Chalcedonians) and "Melkites" ("the king's men," as coined by the Syrians for the Chalcedonians) raged.

Empress Theodora I was sympathetic toward the persecuted churches who rejected the Council of Chalcedon and was instrumental in assisting a dedicated monk, Jacob Baradaeus, to receive consecration as a general metropolitan by Patriarch Theodosius. He was called "Baradaeus," or "the Ragged," because to avoid arrest he wore the disguise of a beggar's clothing as he wandered for more than thirty years throughout the Middle East, ordaining priests and deacons for the non-Chalcedonians. Thus a parallel hierarchy of non-Chalcedonians was sustained, both Chalcedonians and pre-Chalcedonians considering themselves Orthodox and accepting the Nicene Creed. Because of the efforts of the monk Jacob, the Syrian Orthodox are sometimes called "Jacobite" Syrians.

After the Arab conquest of Syria in the seventh century many Syrians became Muslims, but the early years of Muslim occupation were a period of religious toleration. Syrian Orthodox enjoyed positions of influence and prestige under the Caliphs, for the Syrian Christians brought much culture and learning. Until the fourteenth century the Syrian Orthodox Church of Antioch flourished, extending missions across Asia into China, but the Mongol invasion of Persia and Mesopotamia under Timur Lane brought slaughter and devastation to the churches. In recent times, during World War I, many Syrian Orthodox fled persecution in Turkey and settled in various parts of the Arab Middle East.

Through the centuries the Roman Catholic Church has repeatedly made overtures to draw the Syrian Orthodox Church under its authority, succeeding briefly with a reconciliation at the Council of Florence in 1442. Conversations and attempts to understand one another in Christian love continue. Especially promising are unity talks between Roman Catholics of the Eastern rite church in India and the Jacobite Syrian Church of India (under the care of the Antiochian Orthodox Church after a vow of separation from the Catholics since a brief reunion in 1599).

Major Doctrines

Doctrine is based upon Holy Scripture and embodied in the Nicene Creed. Christ's true Godhead and his humanity were essentially united at his Incarnation. The Holy Spirit is confessed to proceed from the Father (no use of the "filioque" clause) and to be the Giver of life to all. Mary is the true Bearer of God, acknowledged to be pure and virginal before, during, and after the birth of Jesus. The Syrian Orthodox Church teaches that there are nine choirs of angels, that at death the souls of the righteous go to Paradise and the wicked to the lowest abyss. Grace is a heavenly gift freely bestowed by God in his mercy and by the merits of Christ, by which we are sustained in working out our salvation, while "justifying grace" is a quality dwelling within the soul importing righteousness to it, making us holy and worthy of eternal life. Sin is understood as "original," embracing humankind as an inheritance from Adam; as deadly, punishable by eternal death; or accidental, doing harm to our spiritual lives.

Geography

Outside the Antiochian See, the church has extended as far as China. Special mention must be made of the Syrian Church of Malabar, or the Syrian Orthodox Church of India, as it is also known. This fully indigenous church is ascribed by tradition to be founded by the apostle St. Thomas, whose place of martyrdom in Mylapore, India, is today a point of pilgrimage. During the early centuries of the growth of the Christian church several groups of Christians and bishops emigrated to India, some of them Nestorians (whose views of the Incarnation were rejected at the Council of Ephesus, prior to the Chalcedon dispute). The history of the Syrian Orthodox Church of India is troubled by struggles for authority, secessions, and controversies that split the church. Colonial Portuguese Catholics, surprised to find over 100 churches already in Malabar, through convening a Synod at Diamper in 1599 tried to bring them under Roman authority, but the Synod was never approved by Rome. Following the murder in 1653 of Bishop Athella, who had been sent by the Patriarch of Antioch, some Syrian Orthodox renounced

Rome and chose Mar Thoma I as their prelate, whom the Patriarch of Antioch regularized. Nine bishops, all named Mar Thoma and of the same family, presided over the Syrian Church until 1817.

Missionaries led the Syrian Church into various changes, or reforms, that split the church, one group eventually becoming part of the Church of South India; another, the "Reformed Syrian Christians," were forerunners of the present Mar Thoma Church. The remaining church was reaffirmed and restructured by the Patriarch of Antioch in Malabar in 1876, but further controversy split the church in 1910 between followers of the Metropolitan of Malabar, who was excommunicated and renamed the catholicos, and those who continued faithful to the Patriarch of Antioch. Repeated efforts to heal the split have been unsuccessful to this day.

Syrian Orthodox of Antioch began to arrive in North America during the late nineteenth century, silk workers from Turkey settling in New Jersey, Turkish weavers in Rhode Island, and others from Syria journeying to Detroit. Other families from Turkey went to Quebec, Canada. The first priest was ordained in the U.S. in 1907, followed by the establishment of several parishes in the eastern U.S. Archbishop Mar Athanasius Yeshae Samuel became the first head of the newly established Archdiocese of the Syrian Orthodox Church in the U.S. and Canada in 1957, and he blessed the St. Mark cathedral in Hackensack, New Jersey, in 1958, consecrating the altars and restored structure in 1972. The building had originally been a Congregational church. A large number of immigrants have passed through St. Mark's lovely and unpretentious cathedral, moving on to help establish the twenty-one parishes of the Archdiocese, including nine from the Syrian Orthodox Church of India.

Organization

The Archdiocese of the Syrian Orthodox Church in the U.S. and Canada is headed by the archbishop; it has approximately 30,000 communicants and is served by twenty-three priests, with two retired pastors. The church accepts apostolic succession from St. Peter, Chief of the Apostles, and looks upon the

Patriarch of Antioch and All the East as his true successor, acknowledging His Holiness as the Supreme Head of the Universal Syrian Orthodox Church and seated upon the Throne of St. Peter of the Holy See of Antioch. The Syrian Orthodox Church of India (Malabar) is affiliated with the Patriarchate of Antioch in ecclesiastical orders, discipline and doctrine, while remaining a fully indigenous church in communion with all the Oriental Orthodox churches. There are about a million and a half followers in each of its two branches, one loyal to the patriarch, the other following another catholicos. The Syrian Orthodox Church of Antioch's Patriarchate is in Damascus, Syria, and the church numbers about two million faithful, with growing communities in Europe, Australia, and the Americas, though it is principally Middle Eastern and Indian. Monastic clergy are the source for episcopal consecrants. The patriarch is elected by the Holy Synod of the Church, composed of metropolitans. Priests may be married prior to ordination, but bishops must be celibate.

Worship

The Divine Liturgy of the Syrian Church of Antioch is the Antiochene type Syrian Liturgy of St. James, and the official liturgical language is Syriac. One of the glories of the Orthodox churches is their liturgy and exalted sense of worship. The Syrians teach and practice the seven traditional sacraments — Baptism (water poured three times over the person in the baptismal font), chrismation (anointing with oil), Holy Eucharist, repentance, matrimony, holy orders, anointing of the sick. Bread and wine in the Eucharist are understood to be transformed or transmuted into the body and blood of Christ. The faithful are daily expected to pray ten *kaumas* in the morning, five at night, hallowing the Sabbath with worship, acts of devotion and service, and refraining from work. *Kaumas* involve the Sign of the Holy Cross, Trinitarian Invocation, prostration, and the Trisagion prayer to the Incarnate Word, concluded by the Lord's Prayer. One may also pray to the Virgin Mary, seeking her intercession and that of the saints, who are respected but not worshipped.

Ecumenical Involvement

The Church is active in the World Council of Churches and the National Council of Churches of Christ in the U.S.. It is in communion with the other Oriental Orthodox pre-Chalcedonian churches.

5

HISTORIC PEACE CHURCHES

CHURCH OF THE BRETHREN

Over the past hundred years the Church of the Brethren has changed more in a shorter period of time than other comparable denominations, according to some observers. It is therefore not surprising that the Brethren of today seem quite different from their historic roots, although many continuities and vestiges remain. Once noticed for their plain dress, they are still honored for their acts of peace and justice.

In the summer of 1708 five men and three women received Baptism in the Eder Brook near the village of Schwarzenau in central Germany. One was Alexander Mack, a close associate of the nobleman and Radical Pietist Hochmann. Mack became a spiritual leader of "the brethren." They had gathered to commit themselves to Christ and to renew and reform Protestantism, which they believed, along with other Pietists, to have become sterile and over-institutionalized. Persecution drove their rapidly expanding group out of Germany, and by 1719 Peter Becker had settled with some of them in Germantown, Pennsylvania, on lands offered free by William Penn. There little notice was taken of "these meek and pious Christians," sometimes called "the Quiet Ones in the Land."

In the American wilderness they established new congregations; one at Conestoga became headed by Conrad Biessel, who quickly determined to go his own way, causing one of the several divisions among them over time. Beissel founded a cloister called Ephrata, which was known for its cultural achievements; it was offered as a military hospital during the Revolutionary War, at which time Beissel's movement ceased. Because they refused to participate in battle, the Brethren suffered at various times during American history, but the church did not sever its internal ties during the Civil War as some communions did. The nineteenth century was a time of consolidation and growth — a congregation was even formed in California by 1858. The Brethren way of evangelism was to live their faith, and many persons were attracted. In 1884 they began a world mission board with $8.69, from which grew outreach to India, Nigeria, China and Ecuador. Today there are almost 100,000 Nigerian Brethren, and an independent Brethren-instituted church exists in Ecuador. They also established schools, six colleges, a seminary, and a Brethren press. Austere, simple living characterized these rural Brethren, but by the turn of the century issues of dress had become vexing. In World War I the Brethren expressed their refusal to bear arms in the Goshen statement, which was painfully withdrawn under the severe threat of treason.

A vigorous concern for peace and active involvement in programs of service and welfare continue as emphases of the Brethren, along with new efforts at evangelism after a serious membership drop beginning in the sixties. Brethren have been leaders in Witness for Peace in Nicaragua, in social justice and service programs (symbolized by the New Windsor, Maryland, relief operation) and in world mission. Many of their efforts, such as the Heifer Project, the Christian Rural Overseas Program (CROP), and the exchange program with the Russian Orthodox Church, have brought vigor and innovation to the ecumenical movement.

Major Doctrines
Brethren affirm "we have no creed but the New Testament, our rule of faith and practice in all things." Although they have a deeply trinitarian theology and find the Nicene Creed compatible, they rarely use creeds in worship. Rather, they look for the norms of faithfulness to Jesus' life and teachings, and to the life,

teachings, and confessions of the early scriptural church and the apostles. The primary focus is commitment to the Word and to reflecting the Word in this world, both through individual experience of God's grace and more ultimately in the community of the church.

Geography

The first Brethren were German, and German background still predominates, although recent outreach has included multiracial groups such as Hispanics, Koreans, Blacks, Haitians, and Filipinos. The Church of the Brethren (the name taken in 1908 after the ultra-conservative Old Order withdrew, taking the German Baptist Brethren name with them) has extended across the nation, but the heaviest concentration of its 160,000 members is still in the upper Midwestern and Mid-Atlantic states (79 percent of total membership). Still more rural than the U.S. population at large, they are also older on the average — with a median age of fifty-four years.

Organization

The Brethren have evolved a blend of congregational autonomy and representative, denominational authority, with an easy two-way flow from congregation to district to Annual Conference. The process is dynamic and sometimes a bit complicated. An individual or group of members may get the support of a congregation to initiate a question or concern, called a *query,* through the district and then the Annual Conference. In 1958 women were approved for full ordination by conference action. The General Board oversees the ministries of the program commissions.

Worship

Because for them every day is sacred, Brethren have been slow to observe the church liturgical year or to observe the Sabbath with special strictness. Meetinghouses brought the congregation together in quiet simplicity, and there also the love feasts were held, after visiting deacons discerned the readiness of the community. The distinctive Brethren love feast includes foot

washing and the kiss of peace, a common agape meal, followed
by the Eucharist around the same tables. Baptism is reserved
for believers prior to confirmation into the church by laying on
of hands. Recently an infant presentation service has also been
introduced. Brethren speak of "ordinances" rather than sacraments, and marriage is an important sacred ceremony. Many
Brethren practice anointing for times of physical or emotional
stress. A prohibition against the swearing of oaths and participation in sacred oath-bound societies is an example of the
Brethren attempt to live scripturally. "Lining out" hymns has
been a common Brethren practice, as has been the wearing of
a prayer veil by women at worship. Ecumenical spirit has introduced new breadth and variety to Brethren worship, but the
most important characteristic of Brethren worship is its inter-
relatedness with the integrity of daily Christian community life
in reconciliation and loving service.

Ecumenical Involvement

The Brethren are members of the World and National Councils of Churches. The church has established a special connection since 1980 with a Pentecostal church in Cuba. After participating as an observer for several years, the Brethren decided in
1966 not to join the Consultation on Church Union, but reaffirmed strongly their attachment to conciliar and cooperative
ecumenism. From the time of their arrival in Germantown, the
Brethren have been close to the Quakers and to the Mennonites
in spirit as well as in geographical proximity, especially in programs of reconciliation and alleviation of suffering in the world.
These "historic peace churches" have provided, in collaboration
with the federal government, civilian work of national importance for religious conscientious objectors.

FRIENDS UNITED MEETING

Just as Christians were first called "Christians" derogatorily at Antioch, so the Quakers were first called "Quaker" as a nickname because they sometimes shook physically or urged others to tremble in the face of the power of the Lord. But they chose to call themselves "Friends," because Jesus said, "You are my friends, if you do what I command you" (John 15:14).

The Friends came into existence in England in the mid-seventeenth century during the Civil War, when Oliver Cromwell brought parliamentary forces to victory. This time of spiritual and political ferment stirred the beginnings of modern democracy even in the church. George Fox, a leather worker with little formal education, sought a more authentic religious vision than the established church provided; in a moment of joyful clarity he heard a voice say, "There is One, even Christ Jesus that can speak to thy condition." His message growing from that encounter stirred other dissenters and "Seekers."

Like a fire ablaze, Friends shared their experience with others; some of them ("The Valiant Sixty") traveled two-by-two throughout the British Isles and across the sea. In 1652 Fox climbed Pendle Hill and saw a vision of a great people waiting to be gathered. Thousands responded, among them Robert Barclay, an intellectual who wrote an *Apology* that still reflects Quaker thinking today. Fox did not intend to found a new religious movement but had hoped to rekindle the church to recover

169

basic Christianity. His fiery verbal encounters provoked violent reactions, and many Quakers suffered serious persecution — imprisonment, confiscation of property, and physical abuse. When new convert William Penn, son of an admiral and associated with the Stuarts, accepted a grant of land in the New World as payment of a debt owed his father by King Charles II, he brought many Quaker settlers to it. This land, Pennsylvania, became the "Holy Experiment" where Quaker principles, including freedom of religion, where applied to government. Rhode Island was the earliest Quaker colony, however, where at one time half the population was Quaker.

The opening of the Northwest Territory as slave-free brought an influx of Friends communities across the country. By 1887 a conference was called in Richmond, Indiana, to gather representatives from various regions in which Yearly Meetings had been established. Seeing the advantages of mutual undertakings, they began to hold conferences at five-year intervals and formally organized as the Five Years Meeting of Friends in America in 1902. The name was changed in 1963 to Friends United Meeting, after which they met triennially.

Quakers have always been concerned with how to live in the world and yet not be taken over by the world. Douglas V. Steere of Haverford College summarizes the early American Quakers in these words:

> Their form of address in using the "thee" and "thou"; their plain clothing; their refusal to remove the hat; their strictness about marrying within the Quaker community; their form of silent worship; their witness against taking any part in wars or in military defense; and, in America, their tenderness to the Indians and later their testimony against the holding of slaves all contributed to making them a "peculiar" people.

The Friends today have discarded many of the practices, but not the spirit they were trying to express. "Far from living behind a wall protected by peculiar customs," says Quaker Elton Trueblood, "contemporary Quakers seek to penetrate the entire

Christian world, somewhat as Fox and Penn sought to do three centuries ago."

Major Doctrines

Rather than shaping a system of thought or creed, Quakers begin with the experience of the presence and the power of the living Christ, who makes his will known and who guides and directs. Christ's presence in the Spirit requires no other mediation, and those who are transformed by Christ pass "from darkness into his glorious light." Friends seek to be "Children of Light" in both personal and social morality. Inwardness, openness, and outwardness are three key characteristics of Quakerism, says A. Burns Chalmers. Quakers would agree with Thomas Carlyle's rugged remark to a new pastor: "What this parish needs is someone who knows God other than by hearsay." Quakers try to make Christ's self-giving love the prevailing spirit of their life and to live in harmony with the creation. The primary Quaker authority is "the Holy Spirit who gave forth the Scriptures."

Geography

Friends United Meeting has a membership of about 60,000 in the U.S. and Canada. There are also 83,000 Friends in East Africa and 800 in Jamaica, Cuba, the West Bank and Mexico. In North America the Friends United Meeting is composed of twelve Yearly Meetings, which are autonomous and authoritative bodies composed of an association of Monthly Meetings that relate geographically. There are also three Yearly Meetings in East Africa and one each in Jamaica and Cuba, for a total of seventeen Yearly Meetings in Friends United Meeting, or over half the world's Quakers.

Organization

Work of Friends United Meeting is done through a General Board and three Commissions: World Ministries, Meeting Ministries, and General Services. Every three years Friends United Meeting convenes in general sessions, and the General Board and its executive committee are interim authoritative bodies.

Friends have no ordained clergy, because only God can ordain, and because the universal ministry involves the priesthood of all believers. There is therefore no question about women also being ministers. Friends do "record" that God has given some Quakers certain gifts or abilities for ministering, and some receive theological education as an enhancement of those gifts. Today pastors serve a large number of Friends Meetings in the United States. Their role is that of servant and not authoritative in the sense of conferred power. Since all are ministers the pastor's task is to stir up and equip the others for their ministry (Ephesians 4:12). Insofar as there is formal leadership or coordination among those Friends who do not have regular pastors, usually called "unprogrammed" Meetings, such leadership is exercised by the clerk (chairperson) of each local Meeting (or congregation).

Worship

Traditionally, expectant waiting upon the Spirit, being open to the presence of Christ, and the breakthrough from isolation into community are the essence of Quaker worship. The use of silence and the experience of being "gathered" into a mystical company releases Christ's transforming power in the lives of those who experience it. However, two-thirds of the North Americans Friends Meetings in Friends United Meeting now are under the leadership of a recorded minister who serves as pastor. The pastor and other Friends that he or she calls upon for assistance generally lead the Meeting for worship. Many Meetings reserve time for unprogrammed or open worship preceding and/or following a prepared message. Generally hymns are sung, Scripture read, prayers offered, and offerings received in much the same way as in other free church traditions. But, as Elton Trueblood notes, when the service is so planned, it is not uncommon for speakers to alter their topics completely, for "even the speakers must never stop listening!"

Ecumenical Involvement

Friends United Meeting participates in the National Council of Churches and the World Council of Churches. The conciliar style of ecumenism is quite distinct from the Quaker consensus mode of decision-making. The lay-clerical dichotomy of other communions, the use of creeds and other structured forms of worship, and the complexity of bureaucracy are hurdles for Quakers, but their commitment to other Christians in Christ's body strengthens their effort. They engage in many dialogues, not only with other Protestants and Roman Catholics, but with other religions as well.

PHILADELPHIA YEARLY MEETING
OF THE RELIGIOUS SOCIETY OF FRIENDS

When George Fox, out of his despair with the religiosity of England in the mid-seventeenth century, discovered the living Christ to be his contemporary, he tapped into a powerful immediacy that spoke strongly to many Christians. By the time of his death in 1691 some fifty to sixty thousand persons in England had become Quakers, as well as large groups in North America and elsewhere.

Mary Fisher and Ann Austin were the first Quaker messengers to the mainland of North America, where they were imprisoned and returned to England. Others who followed them suffered similar persecution — banishment, fines, whippings, imprisonment, even hanging. Mary Dyer was hanged on Boston Common around 1660, the first woman in North America to die for her faith. Yet the Friends prospered, especially in Rhode Island, North Carolina, and Pennsylvania, which was given to Quaker convert William Penn in repayment of a debt.

Quakers distinguished themselves both in deeds and in the life of the spirit. Believing that the Holy Spirit could speak in those who knew nothing of the historical Jesus, they treated the Native Americans as friends and purchased land from them at a fair price. Where treaties were made, they honored them. At a time when many other Christians had few qualms about slavery, many Friends refused to own slaves and are known for their

active role in the Underground Railroad and outspokenness for
abolition. From the 1700s onward, Friends have been active
in the reform of prisons and mental hospitals. Today many
are involved with the sanctuary movement. Founders of distinguished Quaker secondary schools and colleges, Friends have
also pioneered the concept of "life-care" communities for the
elderly. Religious pacifists, their resistance to militarism and to
participation in war has tested the Quaker community numerous times throughout American history. The American Friends
Service Committee, with its active reconciling role in the face
of hostilities, has won respect even from those who do not share
its approach.

Rufus Jones, in a description of his childhood on a farm in
Maine, describes well the spirituality of a Quaker family:

> We never ate a meal which did not begin with a hush of
> thanksgiving; we never began a day without a "family gath-
> ering" at which mother read a chapter of the Bible, af-
> ter which there would follow a weighty silence.... There
> was work inside and outside the house, waiting to be
> done, and yet we sat there hushed and quiet, doing noth-
> ing.... Someone would bow and talk with God so simply
> that He never seemed far away.

As a community of faith, the Quakers take with full seriousness Jesus' promise, "Where two or three are gathered together in my name, there am I in the midst" (Matt. 18:20). In
quiet "centering" the group awaits a word, expressed either "inwardly" or in such spoken words as the Spirit may prompt in
any person present. Philadelphia Yearly Meeting emphasizes
the "non-programmed" approach to worship. Word and deed in
worship are not meant to be separate. John Woolman, Quaker
mystic and early anti-slavery witness whose *Journal* is widely
read, describes this connection:

> In the Lord Jehovah is everlasting strength, and as the
> mind by a humble resignation is united to him and we ut-
> ter words from an inward knowledge that they arise from

the heavenly spring, though our way may be difficult and require close attention to keep in it, and though the manner in which we may be led many tend to our own abasement, yet if we continue in patience and meekness, heavenly peace is the reward of our labours.

People are drawn to the Religious Society of Friends, says Douglas V. Steere, "through a number of doors: the form of worship, the commitment to simplicity in life-style, the accent on religious experience rather than creeds, the peace witness, and the implemented concern for the troubled areas of the world which the service bodies of the Society seek to serve."

Major Doctrines

Although Quakers reject written creeds, they have a religious framework that informs their worship. The idea of the immanence of God is central. God is understood as a loving, creative Spirit resident in all people, suffering with them, developing loving relationships, and working with them toward the realization of a just and good society. Friends believe that this indwelling God continues revelation, that revelation did not cease "when John laid down his pen at Patmos." God is also transcendent. Although traditional Christian orthodox thought is usually employed, the concept of the Indwelling Spirit — or "Light" as Friends speak of it — lends itself to contemporary Christian reinterpretations, such as Paul Tillich's understanding of God as ground and depth of being. Jesus is the highest or deepest realization of this Inner Light, "which enlighteneth everyone who comes into the world." The Christ, whom Friends called the "Royal Seed," guides Friends in every generation as they see the new implications of the Christian revelation.

Geography

In the Religious Society of Friends membership and authority reside with the local congregation or meeting, called a "monthly meeting" because it meets monthly for business. Monthly Meetings in a region form a Yearly Meeting. There are 102 Monthly Meetings in the Philadelphia Yearly Meeting with a total membership of 13,150 Friends in a four-state area. The Philadelphia Yearly Meeting is affiliated with the Friends General Conference, whose headquarters is also in Philadelphia. There are about 31,600 members of the Friends General Conference in over 500 churches.

Organization

It is not surprising that, doctrine being unconfined by a written creed, there should arise different schools of thought and practice. Friends General Conference, of which the Philadelphia Yearly Meeting is a major member, was established in 1900. Seven Yearly Meetings with what might be described as a "liberal" bent originally formed the Friends General Conference. It is presently composed of fourteen Yearly Meetings, five of which hold membership jointly in Friends United Meeting, itself organized in 1902. Since 1950 the FGC has broadened to include orthodox, conservative, and evangelical groups. There are also an Evangelical Friends Alliance composed of four Yearly Meetings, a conservative group of three Yearly Meetings, and seven unaffiliated Yearly Meetings. Friends United Meeting, whose offices are in Richmond, Indiana, where the first gathering of its confederation met, emphasizes a united Quaker witness in missions, peace work, and Christian education, and holds a moderating middle ground. Most of its meetings are "programmed," which in Friends parlance means they have paid pastors and follow a worship format with an order of service not greatly different from other Protestant free churches.

Worship

Friends believe worship happens most powerfully when worship in solitude and worship in community are combined. They sense that they are "gathered" when the Spirit brings a feeling of love and unity beyond human orchestration. Inseparable from this conception of worship is a ministry that is seen as a function, not a profession. For Quakers the distinction between cleric and layperson is considered a destructive human accretion not taught by Jesus. All Christ's followers, men and women equally, are "ordained" and, in the Spirit, have access to the gifts and graces of ministry. When the strivings of the Spirit are felt within them, Friends may find themselves "under concern" to bear witness and to accept obligations "for Truth's sake." To resist or to disobey such "inward promptings" is to crush the Spirit and crucify Christ afresh. As the adherent practices responsiveness to these "leadings," the Light of Christ grows stronger and gives power over adversity and peace to the soul.

Ecumenical Involvement

The Philadelphia Yearly Meeting has been a member of the National Council of Churches since its beginnings in 1950. Through the Friends General Conference it is also a participant in the World Council of Churches. The Friends also strive to forge closer ties with their own separated groups, and seek dialogue with many religious bodies.